WHERE
TWO OR THREE
ARE GATHERED

— ● —

WHERE TWO OR THREE ARE GATHERED

Community Life for the Contemporary Religious

BARBARA FIAND

— • —

CROSSROAD • NEW YORK

This printing: 2000

The Crossroad Publishing Company
370 Lexington Avenue, New York, NY 10017

Copyright © 1992 by Barbara Fiand

Printed in the United States of America
Typesetting output: TEXSource, Houston

Library of Congress Cataloging-in-Publication Data

Fiand, Barbara
    Where two or three are gathered : community life for the
contemporary religious / Barbara Fiand.
        p. cm.
    ISBN 0-8245-1151-4
    1. Monastic and religious life. I. Title.
BX2435.F49 1992
255–dc20   91-36096
                                                           CIP

To KAY
with love and hope

Contents

PREFACE   9

1 AWAITING THE DAWN   13

    Transformative Elements   15

    The Need for Realism   16

    Developmental Parallels   18

    Religious Parallels   26

    Conclusion   29

2 HONORING THE PROCESS   33

    Subtle Dependency Patterns   34

    Facing Our Darkness   38

    Empowerment toward Community   45

    Enduring the Pain of Transition   50

3 RELATIONAL JUSTICE   57

    The Urge toward Obligation   58

    The Need for Liberation   63

4 THE LOVE OF CHRIST IMPELS US   69

   A Call to Conversion   71

   Revolution Not Rebellion   74

Conclusion
SOME THOUGHTS FOR THE NOW   83

   "Sniffing-out" Time   83

   Stability and Space   87

   It Has Everything to Do with Kindness   91

QUESTIONS FOR FOCUS, REFLECTION,
AND DISCUSSION   95

   1 / Awaiting the Dawn   95

   2 / Honoring the Process   96

   3 / Relational Justice   99

   4 / The Love of Christ Impels Us   101

   Conclusion / Some Thoughts for the Now   102

NOTES   105

PREFACE

Not long ago a friend of mine shared with me the following fantasy: "I saw myself at the end of my earthly existence standing before the pearly gates. The guardian of heaven wanted an account of my record. Humbly I began to tell him about my life. To my surprise, however, I did not get much of a chance to outline my achievements, for no sooner had I mentioned that I had spent most of my years on earth living in community, then the heavenly trumpets began to blast triumphantly, choirs of angels broke out in chants of praise, and Peter bowing profusely ushered me straight before the throne of God." We both laughed heartily at her fantasy, for we knew all too well what it implied. We also knew that laughter, at times, helps us endure great sadness.

Why is it that what ought to empower us and give us strength for the mission of Jesus so frequently deprives us of even basic adult necessities? What has happened to community life that for so many of us it has come to be seen as something that must be endured, rather than as an essential part of our life, as something that empowers us, as something we can truly enjoy? Of all the concerns addressing religious congregations in the late twentieth century our seemingly uninspiring life together is, I believe, one of the most urgent, yet also one of the most illusive problems. Ever since the publication of *Living the Vision* in the spring of 1990, I have been astounded by the urgency with which religious throughout this country have responded to my reflections on "Community for Mission." Although the book concerns itself with all three of the evangelical counsels and stresses the primacy of disposition in our vowed commitment as a whole, it was chapter 4, with its emphasis on communal loving, that brought the most frequent responses, together with requests for more in-depth discussion, lectures, workshops, and writings on community life. This book is an attempt to respond to these requests.

It is an *attempt*, and should in no way be construed as anything more than that. The issues we are dealing with call for collective wisdom and require some hard work for all of us. No one person can claim the vision for a common quest. I offer these pages, therefore, merely as my contribution. The questions offered at the end of the book are seen as means toward getting us all more deeply involved. None of us can afford to withhold our wisdom.

I am reminded here of a recent television interview with General Norman Schwartzkopf of Gulf War fame. During their discussion Barbara Walters asked the general whether as a young officer after the Vietnam tragedy he had ever been tempted to quit; whether the nation's and his own discouragement with the failure of that war would not have justified such a choice. "When things are broken and the situation is a mess," the general replied, "then is not the time to quit. The time to leave comes when everything is running smoothly." Though the activity of war is ever repugnant to me, the general's response impressed me. I believe it applies remarkably well (though clearly in a different context) to our present situation in religious life. There are many ways to "quit." Closing ourselves down is hardly the option most of us would choose, but one can "quit" also by refusing to look, to face issues, to acknowledge difficulties. One can "quit" by busying oneself with the nonconsequential and staying with surface concerns. One can "quit" by transferring blame, by discouraged resignation, by refusing to grow. The numerous lectures and workshops addressing our life together that are asked for all over this country, in Canada, and abroad, often at the request of the grassroots membership itself, are a sign to me that for many of us it isn't time to "quit" yet; that we are ready and willing to acknowledge our dilemma and to deal with it. This book is my contribution to the effort.

It is my hope that the reflections presented here will prove of value to religious generally, regardless of their background. The beginning sections of this book, however, do have some areas of difficulty unavoidable if we are to gain a clearer picture of the reasons for the relational turmoil we are presently experiencing. To discuss the parallels that exist between individual, institutional, and cultural development necessitates the use of language and concepts that may not be readily familiar to all. This can prove discouraging. I am aware of this and have attempted to present these concepts as readably as possible. The diagrams in chapter 1 give an overview of the matter under discussion and an easy comparison of the modes of consciousness being considered. The material covered here will provide the reader with the foundations necessary for an appreciation of the relational justice issues discussed in later pages. I would ask the reader, therefore, not to pass over it to move on to more appealing sections of the book, since references to the beginning are made throughout the text.

This is a little volume and must be accepted as that. It does not aspire to address the topic of community life comprehensively. It is an essay, whose origin I owe for the most part to the Leadership Conference of Women Religious (Region 6) who first requested that I draw the thoughts presented here together in an organized fashion. It is a synthesis of workshops and lectures I have given since then throughout the country, a gathering together of my thoughts and the advice, "feedback," and challenge I have received from participants at these workshops and from friends. I owe them all much thanks. My gratitude in this regard goes in a very special way to Clare Gebhardt whose wisdom, gained through many years of community living, as well as through facilitation and consulting work with numerous communities of both men and women, largely inspired my writing. Much thanks goes also to Peggy Nichols and Margaret Fitzer of the Religious Formation Conference who so faithfully invited and organized my lectures throughout this country; to Crossroad Publishing Company for suggesting that I write on this topic and for, once again, generously supporting my efforts; to my friends who helped with the typing and proof reading; and last but not least, to Mary Ann Barnhorn for her faith and for her encouragement.

— I —

AWAITING THE DAWN

When a culture, an institution, or even an individual person is in crisis, the offer of a way out is useless. All answers held forth in an effort to solve the difficulties or assuage the pain of the situation are simply too simplistic and will in the long run only compound the dilemma. A crisis is not solved and cannot be approached like a problem. Strictly speaking, one does not *have* a crisis; rather, one *is in* a crisis. It is of existential significance,[1] and, if properly approached, it will reveal itself as not at all negative or destructive, albeit painful, but rather as part of the very fiber of the human condition itself. A crisis is a turning point of vision that befalls us. It is not something we plan to get into, or decide to get out of. Rather, it is an event that calls us toward transformation very often in spite of ourselves. We ignore it only at our own peril. A crisis challenges us. Whatever it touches it changes. To make it a growthful part of our existence it needs to be faced, to be embraced, and then to be lived through.

In *Living the Vision* I explored the fact that our culture is in crisis and that religious life, as being part of this culture, is caught in the throes of its crisis as well. It is my conviction that community life, as the heart of our congregational existence, is experiencing this crisis most acutely and that in many respects the way we face it, embrace it, and then live through it will determine not only where we will be in the twenty-first century, but whether we will be at all. No one book, of course, can offer an answer to our difficulties and our pain. To assume this would be not only blindly arrogant, but also counterproductive. As I mentioned already, singular solutions here are quite impossible. All of us are caught in the turning point of religious life. All of us are called, therefore, to surrender ourselves to its questions, to live into its darkness, and to await the dawn. The wisdom that will emerge there will have to be our collective wisdom. Our strength, as I see it, will be in creative waiting — serving the truth of our lived reality without fear and in the conviction that what is happening is necessary for the transformation to which we are all called.

My intention, then, in the following pages, will be to expand what I started in *Living the Vision*, much as I have done it in the workshops I have given throughout the country since its publication: to keep probing into the issues and asking the questions that I see as conducive to helping all of us face the crisis and allowing all of us to move toward authentic and life-giving change.

TRANSFORMATIVE ELEMENTS

Recently I was asked to address one of the Midwest chapters of the Leadership Conference of Women Religious (L.C.W.R.). Our reflection centered around "Community Building for Us as Vowed Religious Nearing the Twenty-first Century." As I was getting ready for the presentation, I looked over the "transformative elements" for religious life, which the 1989 joint assembly of the L.C.W.R. and the Conference of Major Superiors of Men had drafted. These were powerful statements, tremendously challenging! My attention focused particularly on elements 1, 4, and 8. Let me here highlight briefly what these elements propose.

Element one proposes that "religious in the year 2010 will serve a prophetic role in the church and society. Living this prophetic witness will include critiquing societal and ecclesial values and structures, calling for systemic change and being converted by the marginalized with whom we serve."

Element four proposes that our spirituality will be a spirituality of wholeness. In the year 2010 we will "live and work in a manner which fosters," among other values: "(a) participation and harmony among all people, (b) healthy personal and interpersonal relationships."

Element eight proposes that communities of the future "will be characterized by inclusivity and intentionality." The list clarifying what is meant by this is extensive:

> Our communities may include persons of different ages, genders, cultures, races, and sexual orientation. They may include persons who are lay or cleric, married or single, as well as vowed and/or unvowed members. . . .

Our communities will be ecumenical, possibly interfaith: faith-sharing will be constitutive of the quality of life in this context of expanded membership. Such inclusivity will necessitate a new understanding of membership and a language to accompany it.

Religious life still includes religious congregations of permanently vowed members.

There is a great deal of hope and promise in what I have just reviewed here. I believe, however, that in the writing of these elements there is even more than that — there is *commitment;* there is *covenant:* "If God is faithful," we say by these proposals, "and God is, then this is how things will be by the year 2010. *This is our pledge!"*

Perhaps looking at things this way can be a frightening proposition. After all, all of us can dream and write vision statements, but "covenant" is a strong word. Many of us may not even be around any longer by the year 2010. Why should we, therefore, have to take on such a burden? Yet, we *will be responsible,* if we speak these transformative elements as vision statements and move them beyond pious platitudes into a *pledge.* What, then, can we do today to fulfill our side of the covenant and to help bring about the vision we have promised to strive for?

THE NEED FOR REALISM

As I see it, to bring about transformation of any kind necessitates a good deal of realism. This means, first of all, that for us as religious today it is essential that we *own* the cultural reality in which we live and *admit our very clear affiliation with it.* Self-proclaimed prophecy is, as we all know, never tremendously effective, and our critiquing of societal and ecclesial values will be creative only within the context of wounded healers — the physicians who are at all times also aware of their own need for healing, of their own brokenness.

It is, I believe, quite obvious that to concentrate on our call to live community participatively, with healthy personal and interpersonal relationships, intentionally, and inclusively is indeed prophetic. It is probably also the one area where most of us are most vulnerable and broken. When it gets to community building and witness, I personally feel very much like Isaiah's "Woe is me, I am doomed! For I am a person of unclean lips, living among a people of unclean lips" (Isa. 6:5). It seems to me that we are really very crippled here and that we desperately need the burning ember of God to touch our hearts and our lips to bring about transformation for the sake of our own personal holiness and then for the sake of witness.

What I am suggesting here is not intended to discourage us or to make us feel guilty in the face of what looks like failure. My intention is, rather, to deal with this issue honestly. For most of us, I am sure, the years of writing and rewriting our constitutions, directories, and community policies have, if nothing else, convinced us that the written word and the enfleshed reality of any situation can be far apart indeed. We have grown suspect (if not publicly then at least in the deep privacy of our own reflections) of "studies," position papers, and idealistic mottos calligraphied above our doorways. It is time, I believe, to move into a more direct confrontation with our dilemma and courageously to embrace ourselves there.

To begin with, it will be of help for us to realize that the directly personal and interdependent mode of relating to which our entire culture is ultimately called seems at present still very much in its embryonic beginnings, if in fact it has even been conceived at all yet. Social psychologists call ours the age of alienation and anxiety.[2] We are a culture whose major relational paradigms are collapsing and it is not at all clear whether, as a society, we have been "emptied out" sufficiently as yet to embrace a more fully human mode of interacting.

I mentioned already that as members of this culture religious are really not too far ahead of it. We are in many respects, especially in the area of relational self-awareness, caught in the very developmental stalemate and confusion that afflict our age and that, if we truly are to critique societal and ecclesial values, we desperately need to transcend. Here the words of Jeremiah's calling come to mind. In all honesty, when it gets to the intricacies of authentic and holistic relating, many of us (along with our culture, rather than counter-culturally as we might like to see ourselves) are indeed "too young" and "know not how to speak" (Jer. 1:6).

DEVELOPMENTAL PARALLELS

To put a bit of flesh on these assertions in order to open up for ourselves possible avenues of transcendence, it may be of value at this point to look more closely at the developmental parallels that can be drawn between the individual and society, as well as between institutional growth and personal maturation.[3]

Individual Development: We all know that as individuals, moving out of the womb into life, we pass through various levels of consciousness. From coenesthesis — a global at-oneness with our mother and, through her, with the entire world — we move into the "terrible twos" and the phase of ego-emergence and individualization that is characterized by over-againstness and separation. This is a time for "independence-from" that culminates ultimately in the height of our abstract capacities and calculative thinking characteristic of adolescence. Whereas the consciousness of coenesthesis is broadly named "biological," the phase of independence and of calculative thinking can perhaps most accurately be identified as "functional" consciousness. During what Bernard J. Boelen calls the "negative phase of adolescence," this mode of consciousness again disintegrates and in due time breaks open to more personal modes of perceiving and relating. Here, in what might best be described as a spiralling movement rather than a linear one, we experience different levels of depth, each with its own "moments of betrayal," its changes and turning points, and its natural drive toward wholeness.

Growing up, as Jungian analyst Edward C. Whitmont puts it, is ever "a road, a way, a process, a travel or *travail*."[4] It is a painful business and has its in-built, its ontological moments of crisis, of disintegration, of death, and of rebirth. Furthermore, each crisis also has its own inherent and quite distinct movements: To begin with, this ontological turning point usually occurs at peak moments of development. Just when we believe that we have life somewhat in order, that we are secure and can relax a little, we mysteriously and quite uncontrollably find ourselves getting restless. Peak experiences do not last in the human momentum toward wholeness and, though they are wonderful and certainly desirable, sooner or later they prove not to be enough any more and we reluctantly find ourselves having to accept Paul's exhortation to the Hebrews: "For here we have no lasting city; we are seeking one which is to come" (Heb. 13:14).

As our securities begin to disintegrate from within, we find ourselves ever more deserted and alone. What spiritual writers call the "dark night" befalls us and leaves us stripped. This is the time that most persons identify as crisis proper, although the turning point has been with them for quite some time already. This also is the time when the desire to escape is the greatest and when, among friends and companions of the sufferer, the temptation to rescue is the strongest. In our personal journeys we will often try to shortcut our stay in the desert by looking for distractions of one kind or another. Nothing is really accomplished that way, however, since a shortcut will only prove to be a detour that will ultimately prolong the agony.

Ontological crises leave us in their *own* time, not according to *our* schedule. At the appointed moment darkness quite literally turns into dawn and a new vision emerges out of our experience of chaos and hopelessness. The time that follows is then usually spent in experimentation with and celebration of the new vision. This can often be a period of radical reform and idealism. It ultimately gives way, however, to a time of more mature integration during which all previous levels of perception and insight are taken in and slowly and thoroughly "re-membered" into the new vision and toward a unified whole. The following is a diagram of the personal development discussed so far:

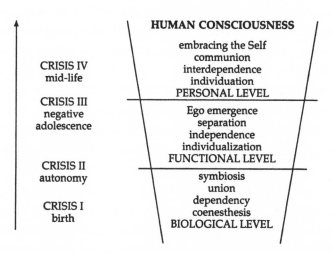

CRISIS IV
mid-life

CRISIS III
negative
adolescence

CRISIS II
autonomy

CRISIS I
birth

HUMAN CONSCIOUSNESS

embracing the Self
communion
interdependence
individuation
PERSONAL LEVEL

Ego emergence
separation
independence
individualization
FUNCTIONAL LEVEL

symbiosis
union
dependency
coenesthesis
BIOLOGICAL LEVEL

The crises indicated to the left of the diagram are the major ontological crises as identified by Boelen. Only the middle two indicate shifts in levels of consciousness. The other two identify major breakthroughs in ways of being within the first and the last level: (1) birth, bringing about physical independence or separation; (2) mid-life, indicating a shift from the first to the second half of life.

Cultural, Institutional Development: Cultures and institutions move toward wholeness much as individuals do, but very much more slowly. Beatrice Bruteau identifies three phases of consciousness in human cultural development. She suggests that Western civilization is at the end of the second and in the crisis of change that, as I have already indicated, always comes with endings and precipitates all new births.

Level I: The first level of consciousness for all cultures appears to have been really very much like the level of coenesthesis in the infant. It was one of union with and absorption into the greater whole. Anthropologists describe it as the age of the "Great Mother." Bruteau calls it the "paleo-feminine era." She situates it as having ended somewhere around 3000 B.C.E. For us, as religious with pre–Vatican II training for the most part, it could be of some interest. It was the age of the clan, the tribe, the "herd mentality." During this period, as Genia Pauli Haddon points out:

> Identity was by inclusion rather than differentiation, the clan or tribal group being the fundamental human unit. Property was communally held. A style of participational consciousness (which has sometimes been called "participation mystique") probably predominated, the process of mental differentiation, objectivity, and division of opposites not yet having become the dominant mode of cognition.[5]

Participational consciousness put individual perception (to the extent to which it even existed) totally at the service of the whole. The unity and survival of the tribe was the ground of all experience and the source of all values. Feelings, emotional patterns, psychic sensitivity, and magic occupied a large part of community life. Separation from the clan almost invariably spelled death. This mode of consciousness is estimated to have lasted about twenty-two thousand years[6] and ended with the emergence of the *hero* — the great *individual.*

Level II: In personal human development this emergence parallels the phase of ego-emergence or the movement from dependence to independence we discussed earlier. For both cultural as well as individual growth the period of individualization along with the consciousness it brings is a very important one. Bruteau identifies it as the "masculine" era of consciousness and has high praise for it:

In the past, confrontation with the huge human environment and the pressure arising not only from the will to survive but from the will to grow, which is characteristic of the human being, made the excluding and focusing consciousness advisable. The range of human senses and human actions, to say nothing of human emotions and human thoughts, is so much greater than that of most animals, . . . that the human world became gigantic. No one person could work effectively in all of it. The separation of a large subject-matter into component parts according to some useful pattern (analysis) and limitation of one's energy, psychic and physical, to some specific area, would seem to have been the only sensible solution.

This *focusing* of consciousness inevitably led to an appreciation of the psychological attitudes necessary to maintain the focus: reinforcement for skill in one's specialty, belief that one's work was a good thing, deserving of honor, . . . camaraderie with others pursuing the same work, refusal to devote one's time or emotional energy to other tasks (which other tasks were therefore scorned or seen as not right for oneself), and so on. This in turn led to the elevation of what we consider the typically masculine virtues: loyalty to one's group; intention to organize affairs — and the whole society if

possible — to one' own advantage, that is, to dominate
other groups, either overtly or subtly; the ability to make
ruthless decisions, and the power to implement them.

... At this point, when the qualities of this age have
been developed to an extreme pitch and we are beginning to sense a shift to another modality, we may be
tempted to concentrate on what we view as its negative
aspects: the aggressiveness, the social stratification, the
dangerous power we possess over the physical, chemi-
cal, and biological agencies of the world. But we should
take great care to remember and to realize that it was
only by cultivating these very processes and the psychic dispositions which supported them that we were
enabled to come to this, the next threshold, where we
see that we can transcend these qualities. [7]

On the individual level of human development this mode
of consciousness is often identified as the level of functional
relating and objective thinking. Bruteau's extensive quotation has provided us with a detailed appraisal of it that is
applicable on the personal level as well. In summary, then,
we can say that in its more advanced aspects, both individually and culturally, this form of consciousness provides us
with independent rational thought, with speculation, theo-
rizing, calculation, the capacity for administrative tasks of all
kinds, for scientific research and strategic planning.

For the last five thousand years it has presided over
human interactions. It is the reason for human progress and
for civilization as we know it today. Pauli Haddon puts it well
when she points out that this mode of consciousness and the
worldview that has flowed from it:

has been humankind's collective story, told and retold in hundreds of variations. Its motifs resound in old fairy tales, in religious myths and institutions, in the scientific attitude and method, in sociopolitical patterns, in family structures, in countless personal life scripts, and in all the major psychological theories. Creating and living this story has benefited humankind in the development of discriminating consciousness and all that follows from it.[8]

Today, we are called not to reject the focusing, individualistic mode of awareness we have been discussing, but to transcend it, and it is here that our energies will need to focus. If diagramed as were the levels of individual human consciousness, cultural development would look somewhat like this:

CULTURAL CONSCIOUSNESS

III
mutuality
communion
holistic consciousness
personal interrelation
dialogue
the future
INTERPERSONAL VALUES

II
social stratification
competition
separation
functional consciousness
rise of the hero, the individual
3000 B.C.E.–1992 C.E.
"MASCULINE" VALUES

I
group dominance
clan mentality
tribal consciousness
25000 B.C.E.–3000 B.C.E.
"PALEO-FEMININE" VALUES

RELIGIOUS PARALLELS

The religious consciousness and subsequent self-expression of any group or institution invariably is rooted in the cultural consciousness of its time. It is helpful, therefore, to observe developmental parallels here.

RELIGIOUS CONSCIOUSNESS

III
inductive theology rooted in praxis
mystical, ecological, holistic orientation
accepting of polarities, paradox
valuing unity in diversity
EXPERIENCE OF GOD IN THE DEPTH
OF THE SELF

II
faith understood as intellectual assent
speculative, deductive theology
dualism: idealism-materialism
SYSTEMATIZATION
OF THE MYSTERY

I
animism
magic
MYSTERY AS
ALL-ENCOMPASSING

The diagram above speaks perhaps more directly to religious and theological development in our Christian tradition than to religious congregational life as such. Nevertheless, we can, I believe, quite readily see our place. We identify ourselves, after all, as "religious," and, therefore, the way the wider religious community addresses the Mystery will also quite naturally be the way we look at the mystery of our lives together.

Level II: It seems clear that the stress we place congregationally on the systematization of our life, on identifying objectives, on strategizing and writing policies, on statistics, on agendas and minutes for our meetings, etc., places us in the middle level of awareness, the level of deduction and speculation, the level of functional values. These concerns are of significance in any organization and ought, of course, not be neglected but if stressed excessively, they can also have us fall prey to what in *Living the Vision* I have called the *Cartesian affliction:* "We write, therefore *it is.*" An undue emphasis here can all too readily have us lose our Gospel perspective and delude us into thinking that policy formation *is* praxis. With functional values looming large we can easily stay at the periphery of things instead of moving into the experience of God in our midst, into the heart of it all. Too many of our chapters and assemblies are, I fear, still bogged down with interminable sessions devoted to identifying objectives and writing mission statements, with procedural squabbles and "politicking," with the commissioning of numerous "studies" that require precious time and rarely achieve the congregational transformation for which they are intended. They have us fulfill the mandates of functionalism and theoretical speculation and, by bringing closure to our work that is otherwise riddled with so much uncertainty, they lull us into the illusion that "something after all is being done about our dilemma."

Nor do facilitators necessarily solve our problem and make our meetings more personal. A process is only as good as the consciousness and the freedom of the facilitator who designed it. And, perhaps, this is precisely the point: *functional* processes *need* to be *designed well ahead of time*, and thus easily pose the danger that, when meetings are held, the participants will be made to *fit* the design. *Personal* processes, however, need to *fit the persons involved in them* and their specific concerns. Like all creative tasks, facilitation is an art that needs to adapt itself to the medium, otherwise the truth cannot appear. Facilitation that is fixed before it starts may be neat but can hardly personalize our interactions. The ability to adapt and move with the depth agenda of the participants (to be distinguished from the written agenda prepared ahead of time) will quite probably be less focused on "task," but it flows from the wisdom of interpersonal relating and knows that any task that does not respect the "maintenance" needs of the participants in the group is ultimately just another lifeless project among the many that are already gathering dust on the shelves of our congregational affairs.

Level I: Regarding our institutional concerns, it may be safe to say that the animistic, magical level of awareness has generally been transcended, except perhaps in isolated cases such as in communities where appointments are still made without consulting the religious involved, and where the "grace of state" is expected to supply for all inadequacies in preparation or in talents. Clan consciousness, however, persists still, I think, in some of our local communities. Dependency issues surface there much more readily and need to be addressed. We will want to look at this more in detail in the next chapter. For the moment, suffice it to say that movement to the relational model of the personal (as different from the functional, analytical model of consciousness to which we have been accustomed for so long, and also as different from the clan mentality in which some of us may still, at times, be embroiled) is truly an invitation to transcendence. In spite of the difficulties and the pain that it will bring, I can see no better place for our witness to this transcendence than in our own communities, for there we will ultimately need to face and work out the unity between community and mission we have all so long been hoping for. To be true to the "transformative elements" we have envisioned for ourselves at our leadership conferences, we will have to make our living together part of our effecting the mission of Jesus; and *who we are*, rather than just *what we do*, will then be charged with liberating energy for this age. But this will not be an easy task, for once again it is here, precisely because we are not different from but a part of our culture, that we need to be very honest.

CONCLUSION

In conclusion, a parallel presentation of the three levels of consciousness discussed in this chapter under the headings of individual "Human," of "Cultural," and, concomitantly, of "Religious" may be of help to the reader (see p. 30).

It is clear that the movements characteristic of an ontological crisis are consciously experienced by an individual, a culture, or an institution only when awareness has been developed sufficiently for this. Later crises (i.e., III and IV) will appear as much more acute, therefore than earlier ones.

At present, our culture, and the large institutions within it, appear to be experiencing themselves in the climax of the second level of consciousness that is ever more steadily proving to be inadequate for their emerging needs. The resultant state of crisis (III) causes general alienation and confusion.

With respect to individuals, it is important to note that, whereas some (though in no way the majority as yet) may

	HUMAN CONSCIOUSNESS	CULTURAL CONSCIOUSNESS	RELIGIOUS CONSCIOUSNESS
CRISIS IV mid-life	embracing the Self communion interdependence individuation **PERSONAL LEVEL**	mutuality communion holistic consciousness personal interrelation dialogue the future **INTERPERSONAL VALUES**	inductive theology rooted in praxis mystical, ecological, holistic orientation accepting of polarities, paradox valuing unity in diversity **EXPERIENCE OF GOD IN THE DEPTH OF THE SELF**
CRISIS III negative adolescence	Ego emergence separation independence individualization **FUNCTIONAL LEVEL**	social stratification competition separation functional consciousness rise of the hero, the individual 3000 B.C.E.–1992 C.E. **"MASCULINE" VALUES**	faith understood as intellectual assent speculative, deductive theology dualism: idealism-materialism **SYSTEMATIZATION OF THE MYSTERY**
CRISIS II autonomy / CRISIS I birth	symbiosis union dependency coenesthesis **BIOLOGICAL LEVEL**	group dominance clan mentality tribal consciousness 25000 B.C.E.–3000 B.C.E. **"PALEO-FEMININE" VALUES**	animism magic **MYSTERY AS ALL-ENCOMPASSING**

have quite readily moved from dependence through independence to interdependence, this growth process can be more painful and may even be hindered if it is not supported by the culture or institution in which they find themselves. This makes it more difficult for individuals to sustain the momentum of growth, and regression is, therefore, frequent.

— 2 —

HONORING THE PROCESS

If we are to liberate community living toward holistic and personal forms of consciousness and witness this to our culture, we need to address issues of maturity and of relational justice in our very midst. In the light of what we have discussed in the preceding chapter, this would require that we look at where in the developmental schema discussed there our individual communities find themselves, and what in our modes of interaction will need to die so that new life can sprout among us.

To begin with, and to keep all of us grounded in the realism so essential for a successful confrontation with the dilemma of our times, it is important to stress how necessary it will be for all of us to commit ourselves to honoring the growth process both individually and communally. By this I mean that we will *consciously* need to give it attention, time, and energy, for there is always the danger that in trying to rush it we will abort it. Furthermore, it will not be enough for us merely to "administer" this process: It is a fallacy to assume that decrees formulated regarding a more enlightened way of community living or inviting an "expert" into our midst to give us a workshop on community life will absolve us from the arduous task of exploring our congregation's or even our own personal movement from dependency through independence to interdependence. Because of the particular history of religious life, this task is particularly complex for us. Workshops, therefore, may be valuable to introduce the topic and to enable us to speak with the same vocabulary, but they never ought to stand on their own. All of us will need to address our existential situation critically and sincerely so that conscientization can be effective, and true growth can take place.

SUBTLE DEPENDENCY PATTERNS

From a psychological perspective persons under stress (and community life has its moments of stress) tend to regress to thought and behavior patterns acquired during childhood trauma and frequently not worked through or dealt with. The dependency-independence journey is in reality never a "once and for all" affair. Given a situation of pressure or difficulty the child victim within can emerge quite readily in most of us and regain energy that ordinarily is no longer appropriate for him or her. This dynamic is particularly confusing for those who are not conscious of it. The causes of stress are manifold. Among them, without doubt, some of the most acute have to do with abrupt change. Radical alterations in a person's lifestyle or bonding and relational patterns, separation from significant others, sudden deprivation of affection — all are conducive to it and can bring with them regressive behavior.

That religious congregations in the past were special havens for this kind of stress is difficult to deny. With entrance requirements that stipulated separation from all that was dear, where in the best tradition of Thomas à Kempis it was expected that one left one's family "behind" when one entered, tension ran rampant and a healthy response to one's new environment is difficult to imagine. Unfortunately the "formation" environment itself also was so unhealthy that regression often went totally unnoticed and was at times even hailed as virtue. In a situation where speaking about home was considered "lack of detachment," where one could visit with one's family only under constraining circumstances, where even the deaths of one's relatives could not be mourned in the appropriate cultural and familial setting, where the expression of feelings was at all times monitored by the rules of religious decorum, where independent thinking was frowned upon and all decisions were made by one's "superiors," there rarely was the opportunity to notice and then to address regressive conduct, let alone to work it through. As a consequence, many of the behavior patterns we developed that today are tolerated if not accepted and that are now often excused as "simply part of community life," may in reality be quite destructive of it, considering authentic adult needs.

In many congregations, furthermore, during the years since Vatican II almost all community energy has been spent in furthering ministry (good as this certainly is in itself), and it was assumed for the most part that the professional education of our members would take care of their maturation as well. But to our dismay we are today still finding religious whose emotional needs and expectations are often no more developed than those of the clan — a hidden "wanting to be taken care of" where the parent looms large. Intellectual growth and professional competence do not guarantee emotional maturation. The sad thing is that most of us neither want to acknowledge this, nor know what to do about the relational poverty in our midst, and often we even quite unconsciously further it.

The concern, for example, about the good opinion of superiors (seemingly still prevalent among so many of us), the need to justify our behavior to them and to get approval from them, the temptation to gossip in the halls of administration in defense of ourselves and, of course, always "for sister's or brother's own good," the unspoken and often unconscious expectation that someone more powerful than oneself will "fix things up" and "set things straight," all speak to the issue of childhood dependency needs not addressed. The excessive preoccupation some of us seem to have with getting our view heard even as we sit silently at community meetings and let others do the talking, passively resenting the attention they are getting and actively criticizing them after the meeting is over and in a forum that appears less threatening to us, also relates to this issue. Persons who have not been legitimately recognized for their gifts and whose childhood needs have not been successfully faced and transcended cannot be expected to communicate directly without experiencing considerable distress.

Dependents expect their guardians to take care of complicated matters, to defend them and speak for them, to monitor disputes and to solve conflicts. To the extent to which we have not adequately navigated beyond and then integrated our own ontological state of dependency we will continue to look to our leadership to assume security roles for us. Leadership that has not matured in its own turn will continue to supply them in the name of service.

Nor does any of this need to be conscious, and herein lies the dilemma: We call our "superiors" our "leadership" now and can easily deceive ourselves that the name will take care of all unnecessary subservience and authoritarianism. We have spent hours upon hours at congregational assemblies working hard at restructuring our government and, for many of us, everything was and now is done by consensus. We can easily reassure ourselves that matters from now on will, therefore, be handled in an "adult" fashion. But what really has changed *within? That* will forever be the decisive question!

The signs of dependency can be quite subtle and can often most easily be found in our language: We expect "pastoral leadership," we say; we want "someone we can talk to"; we want our leadership to "do something about our lives." We speak the vocabulary of in-built dependency. The satisfaction of our security needs, moreover, does not have to be centered in one person or even in a team. It can just as easily focus on the whole group, particularly if, unaware of the real source of our needs, we attempt to assuage them by proclaiming consensual governance, and then find ourselves, under the guise of "discussion," browbeating each other and even ourselves into agreeing with the majority.

Although we are truly professionals in our ministries, many of us have never really allowed ourselves, or been allowed, to move from the clan mentality of pre–Vatican II concepts of community to personal independence and, onward, to the interdependent ways of relating with each other where dysfunctional behavior patterns can be detected more clearly, can be addressed, and then healed. The tragedy is that because we have so effectively succeeded in clothing our unanswered childhood needs in adult vocabulary and concepts, we are now hard pressed and even reluctant to recognize them. Whether we like it or not, however, what Sandra Schneiders calls the "primary family model"[9] still pervades many of our communities, and most of us claim to be too busy about ministry needs and mission statements, about administration and corporate affairs to do anything about it. As a consequence, with respect to community life, our myths are collapsing and we find ourselves in a phase of radical doubt.

FACING OUR DARKNESS

The tensions and difficulties in our life together do not go away when we refuse to look at them; nor can they be dealt with purely administratively. Unfortunate though this may be, it is incorrect to assume that scheduled community meetings, valuable though they are, will take care of our relational poverty. When people have not learned to interrelate with each other, to address personal issues in personal ways and individual issues in private settings, community meetings can become battlegrounds where all possible aggression is dumped either overtly or through passive manipulation. They can also become "gang rape" sessions where the community scapegoat gets systematically slaughtered.

When persons have not learned to acknowledge their inner needs, let alone address them, they unconsciously find someone to blame for their frustrations. Invariably the talented, the different, the sensitive personality gets "zeroed-in on," and then, tragically, when these persons leave the congregation or choose to live alone, we wonder whether they were meant for religious life in the first place and absolve ourselves from all blame.

It is of tremendous importance for us to take seriously Mary Wolff-Salin's observation that "we all come into community life, as into marriage, carrying images from the past still insufficiently integrated. Learning not to project these onto others is a long process."[10] I have developed this point more extensively in *Living the Vision*. Suffice it to say here that we ignore this process only at our own peril. If we come from dysfunctional family settings, and it is estimated that most of us do,[11] and if we have not had the chance to address our consequent dysfunctional patterns of behavior, we will bring them with us and we will act them out in community.

Wolff-Salin identifies authority figures as the easiest targets for our projections. She points out, however, that other persons, particularly those who are or appear powerful or gifted or who are leaders, but also those who are manipulative or who are different from the majority, are very easy replacements for "authority" figures properly so called. This is especially the case today when "community" is so frequently a living arrangement of peers. In this setting, perhaps more than anywhere else, we need to be aware of the danger of scapegoating. Our peers can easily become the targets of our unacknowledged and often unconscious expectations and then, when they do not meet these, they can just as easily be ostracized and victimized.

When needs and desires, as well as one's own inner propensity for evil, are unconscious, it is not uncommon that persons are condemned for one thing, while the issue is really quite another. This is why Jung lays such stress on our call to individuation, on our need to bring to consciousness what lies hidden and repressed, on the importance of discovering the shadow dimensions of our own personality and thus being enabled to acknowledge our own potential for darkness. Much suffering and injustice can be avoided in our communal interactions if we do.

There are numerous ways to help us identify shadow material and bring to consciousness our projections. Jung, of course, stresses dreams as one of the richest sources. In significant dreams all personalities can be seen as one aspect or another of our personality, but shadow aspects generally appear as unattractive, repulsive, "inferior" persons of the same gender as the dreamer. These shadow personalities can be strangers, but may also be acquaintances. They can be figures from fairy tales, television, books one has read; they may be public enemies, social outcasts, persons physically disfigured — symbolizing inner disfigurement.[12] The way they appear in one's dream and what they arouse in the dreamer will have valuable information about his or her own repressed and unacknowledged propensity for evil and should not be dismissed lightly as "just a dream."

Fantasies can also be rich in shadow material. It is interesting to observe how ready most of us are to share our dreams;

after all, their content is not of our choosing. But fantasies are different. Many persons fantasize behavior they would never allow themselves consciously to engage in. Sometimes they may even have other persons perform these actions in their fantasies, while they take a kind of voyeuristic enjoyment in them, thus repressing their own connectedness to the deed even further. This is where Jung sees the possibility for detecting our potential darkness. Nothing is "just" a fantasy. There is a greater wealth than we suspect in our mental meanderings. Thus, a young seminarian who habitually fancies himself adorned with crozier and miter as he presides over the assembly, or who sees himself strolling through the halls of the Vatican decked out in red or white, may need to reflect on the hidden motivation behind his "vocation" and question whether indeed the reign of God is uppermost in his mind. His fantasies hold a powerful message for him.

What arouses severe disdain or anger in us, what scandalizes us and has us speak about it to others with self-righteous horror, most likely is shadow material as well. Here the issue is not in the initial negative reaction to another person's lack of virtue or even sin; it lies, rather, in the intensity of affect accompanying our reaction. It is not *that* one is angry or upset, but why one is *so* upset that usually reveals unconscious agenda.[13] Along the same vein, the intensity of denial when our own sins or shortcomings are pointed out to us may be indicative of their possible accuracy as well. Usually when we are falsely accused there may be initial amazement or hurt; we might want clearer examples and may even request that the offense, if it reoccurs, be pointed out to us so that we might become more aware of it. Such reactions are quite normal. When, however, we protest too vehemently without time for any reflection, when we cannot stop talking about the accusation and its injustice, the "too much" in our reaction may be a sign of the observation's validity.

What are innocently referred to as "slips of the tongue" can also at times help us discover the real nature of our actions. John A. Sanford recounts the example of "the good 'Christian' woman ... who was furiously angry with another woman but could not face it. She declared, ... 'I spoke to her *venom*ently.' Of course she meant to say vehemently, but it came out venomently, and venom is actually what she had in her heart toward this person, but she had been unable to recognize the fact."[14]

Finally, laughter at inappropriate behavior — amusement with sin, with cruelty, or unkindness, with sarcasm or meanness — generally indicates one's hidden propensity for the same. More innocently put:

> An analysis of humor shows that it is usually the shadow personality who laughs. This is because humor expresses so many of our hidden, inferior, or feared emotions. For this reason another way to get at a knowledge of our Shadow is to observe what it is that strikes our sense of humor, for in our laughter we can often see our shadow being harmlessly released.[15]

Among religious it is perhaps especially necessary that the shadow be taken seriously, for the training we received in the "ways of perfection" probably makes it particularly difficult for us in spite of our acts of humility to face our shortcomings. When one feels called to be perfect one can actually begin to believe that such a thing is possible. This makes every failure doubly frustrating and painful and the temptation to deny it all the more pressing. It would seem to me much more healing for all of us if we strove for compassion and left perfection where it truly belongs — in the heart of God.

It may be important to stress at this point that the necessity to face our inner darkness ought not be misconstrued as an exercise in self-deprecation. We face our shadow above all else to free its repressed positive energies. The scope of this book does not permit a lengthy discussion on the nature of socialization and on the repression and subsequent persona formation that invariably accompany all attempts at becoming acceptable to the world in which one grows up. Suffice it to say that all of us during our childhood years became relative strangers to a great portion of our personality that, for whatever reason, did not fit into the environment in which we were raised. Maturation, what Jung calls "individuation," requires that during our adult years we reacquaint ourselves with this dimension of ourselves, for in it lies hidden much potential for good.

In my own discussions on detecting the shadow I always stress the importance of not being too ashamed and of being curious instead. If we truly believe that "God saw that it was good" when God created us, then we will have to accept that the root energy of the human being is good. The shadow distorts what was originally good. If we can, therefore, get to the root energy after we have faced the darkness within, we might be able to liberate it and supply ourselves with much needed momentum for growth.

An illustration may be helpful here: If one were, for example, to discover a shadow dimension of one's personality to be sarcasm, it would be helpful, even though painful perhaps, to probe into the "gift" that lies hidden there. In this way one would discover that the root energy that is distorted in sarcasm could really be very beneficial: Sarcasm is built on the capacity to detect weakness that is misused to hurt others. But this power can be used not only for embarrassing someone by exposing that weakness and humiliating him or her, but also for empowerment of the other, for building up and encouragement. The repressed energy of the shadow has lain fallow since early childhood, thus benefiting no one. It also may have been projected negatively onto others, or exercised in the form of sarcasm that was subsequently denied. Now in the discovery of the root potential, it can be liberated for the good. Freedom, as Erich Fromm rightly defines it, is "acting on the basis of the awareness of alternatives and their consequences."[16] Discovering our inner darkness and thus bringing it to light presents us with an alternative to it and in this way frees us to use its energy toward the good.

There can be no doubt that the liberation of the shadow can be of immense benefit to community life. Moreover, living in community provides us with an excellent opportunity for working out shadow issues. Our day-to-day interactions, removed from "professional" surroundings, our rubbing of elbows, if you will, brings to the fore our weaknesses and vulnerabilities and invites us to face them. The fact remains, however, that doing so is by no means a pleasant experience. It is at all times a slow and arduous project that requires dedication to one's inner journey and a great commitment to honesty. Nor can this commitment be made by all the members of the community together (at community goal setting, for example). Encountering the shadow is a very delicate, personal affair. In many respects I see the shadow as the gatekeeper of the second journey, as the herald of crisis IV mentioned in the previous chapter, and very definitely as capable of discovery only within the realms of personal consciousness. And this is precisely where our difficulty lies. The clan concept of community still looms large for a great number of us and, as I mentioned already, subtle dependency patterns and a propensity for scapegoating continue to prevail in our interpersonal ways of relating. Only a strongly identified ego can endure the onslaught of persona disintegration. If, therefore, security issues remain our primary concern, the energy that could be released through the discovery of our individual and even our collective shadow may be unavailable to most of us as yet.

EMPOWERMENT TOWARD COMMUNITY

What then can we realistically expect from our leadership and from each other with regard to community building and a movement beyond the clan? To begin with, it would seem to me that leaders of a group honor their role as leaders only to the extent to which they call the group to concern itself with what the group has claimed as its concerns. As obvious as this may seem, it is clearly not always an easy or a gratifying ministry. To help implement constitutional commitments can be extremely unsettling. Ideals are much more readily professed than put into practice, but leaders are worth their calling only to the extent to which they take the group seriously and, therefore, empower the group to be about what the group says the group wants to be about.

If we say we are about community building, and, as one of the sisters in my own congregation suggested, the cry everywhere seems to point to this almost as if we were in quest of the Holy Grail, then to begin with some clarifying sessions concerning expectations vis-à-vis community and its different meaning for each of us will need to happen among us. Numerous indeed are the occasions when statements such as these are made: "If we were *really* a community, then we would do such and such"; "If *she* understood community, then she would not do such and such"; "We just don't have *real* community in this house." If at that time a clarification were asked for from the speaker and dialogue about expectations regarding community were encouraged, much misunderstanding might be averted. We simply do not all agree about what community is, nor do we all have the same needs in community, but often we *assume* we do.

For someone who is still desiring to be taken care of, for another who unofficially nominates a member of the group to be the focal point around which the community "gels," for still another whose authority issues have never been addressed and who sees in every suggestion, innocently made, an "order" against which our "modern" understanding of "collegiality" compels us to take a stand, for a fourth who expects intimacy as a *right* and who sees in every other friendship a threat to her or his inclusion, much of what adults can reasonably expect of each other in community will prove disappointing.

It is my sense that too often in situations such as these leadership will still feel the urge (or be expected) to come to the rescue of the complainer and to rectify matters to suit his or her needs. One of the worst times for this is, of course, during community meetings, yet these are frequently perceived to be the only occasions when direct communication is possible. There, under the protection of a facilitator, a member of the leadership group, or even one's friends, sufficient safety is experienced to voice one's views and to criticize often totally unsuspecting offenders. This is clearly a "clan" form of behavior, which situates us right back in Schneiders's primary family model, but often it goes unrecognized as such and is in fact encouraged. Because hitherto silent religious are in such a setting "able" to talk, their behavior is misinterpreted as adult and the inappropriateness of the situation or of the issue is often ignored.

If one member of a community finds another member problematic, he or she needs to be encouraged to speak to this person directly. Speaking to authority should never be perceived as being the solution. Adults need to solve their own issues. Too often leadership allow themselves to be put into the uncomfortable position of (a) having to guard confidentiality, and (b) being expected to solve a relational concern. Because of "a" they can never really get both sides of the story and can therefore quite easily lose their objectivity; because of "b" they are put into a parental role that is not and ought not to be theirs in the first place.

A gentle refusal both with respect to guarding confidentiality and with respect to solving the relational concern seems the best solution here. Otherwise authority positions can quite easily turn into sanctioned gossip centers rather than agencies of empowerment toward growth. Practically the matter could be handled quite simply:

1. Insist that unless you can be permitted to mediate a dialogue between both parties, it is quite useless to bring the

matter to you. Here leadership needs to be particularly in touch with personal shadow material. None of us is immune from the desire to get the "scoop" and be on the inside track of information. Furthermore, the sister's or brother's stature in the congregation, our friendship with him or her, our own need to be liked, to be popular, or quite simply our need to "take care of " or "rescue" others can all play havoc with our mandate to empower mature, adult interactions.

2. Never accept at face value the naming of other members in the community as agreeing with the complainer. Insist that you will need to hear from each of them, and negotiate discussion with the offending member and each other person involved if necessary.

Following these two simple rules will have the following consequences: First, and most importantly, it will force people to face their own integrity instead of counting on others to act on their behalf. This and this alone will bring about mature interaction. It will perhaps initially cause great consternation, for there are few communities where what I have suggested is common practice. Somehow it does not fit into what we have commonly understood as "pastoral" leadership. Those who implement these rules of intervention may, therefore, not be popular at the beginning. Empowering persons to face their own integrity, however, can in the long run only be for their benefit and wholeness.

The second consequence of insisting on mediation and calling each affected member to participate in the dialogue is that it will foster direct communication. When there is no one to speak for us and to take care of our concerns, we will finally have to do it for ourselves. It might be of value to point out here that the membership as well and not only the leadership in religious congregations needs to be aware of these relational requirements. "Third-person communication" is merely the replacement of named authority by some other power and is equally debilitating in the struggle to build mature communities. Nor should the excuse of "merely letting off steam" be taken too seriously. It is true that most of us need to do this at times, but it also is true that the "sins of the tongue" are rampant in community life and contribute largely to our failure to live this life effectively. Furthermore, it is quite possible that unconsciously we really do want the "third" person to help us out in this matter and use the excuse of "letting off steam" merely to communicate our dilemma.

Lastly, mediation and direct dialogue between affected members prevent the scapegoating of any member by the group and allow the person to speak to the issue in an environment that is suited to the issue. Personal affairs should be handled in personal settings, and the proper forum for individual differences is the private forum. Clan attacks belong to another era.

Now all of us are very busy people and so are the administrators of our institutions. The approach recommended here takes time, devotion, and skill. It is my conviction, however, that it is extremely important. If leadership does not have time for this, therefore, I would strongly urge the full delegation of this matter to a qualified person who can handle it. It is of little value to delegate this kind of work only partially — to listen to the complaint but not to execute the dialogue. Such behavior gives false messages and only encourages gossip and childishness.

Many a religious has moved away from community life or, for that matter, from religious life altogether, because she or he could no longer stand the heavy-duty atmosphere of unvoiced irritation, unrecognized expectations, and passive aggression. These same dysfunctional behavior patterns, by the way, could also have been his or hers. The mode of our interactions, however, has not encouraged any of us to face this. Our stress level in this age is very high. As I have suggested already, this is largely due to the turning point or crisis in which we find ourselves as a culture. Community needs to be a place where we can grow without threat. Otherwise it betrays the drive toward individuation that is ontologically ours. If we cannot mature in communal settings we have no right to proclaim ours as a "way toward holiness," and we would do a disservice to those whom we encourage to join us.

ENDURING THE PAIN OF TRANSITION

The issues discussed in the preceding pages address our fixations at the "clan" level of consciousness, where many of us have remained communally since Vatican II. The need here for creative growth toward deeper, more open forms of consciousness is clear. The matter, however, is not resolved with the transcendence of clan dependency alone. Mature interrelationships happen on the level of the *personal*, where interdependence has become a conscious value. Although nothing short of this will do, it is nevertheless a fact that a prior level of consciousness needs to be navigated first before this can come about.

Difficult as it may be for us to accept, the laws of human maturation are such that levels of growth cannot be skipped.

We are dealing here with ontological modes of seeing: levels of awareness that open up to each other, one, if you will, surrendering to the next and then being taken up into it, toward ever deeper levels of integration. Interdependence is not possible for someone who has not experienced independence. The interplay between assertion and yielding that is essential for authentic adult interaction necessitates a strong ego and a secure sense of identity. Otherwise what is intended to be communion turns into absorption and we find ourselves back once more in the herdal mode of relating we believed ourselves to have outgrown.

The urge (mostly unconscious because unrecognized) toward "level skipping" was in many respects what most of us faced in the years shortly after Vatican II. Having been firmly established in behavior patterns of the "primary" family model and of the clan dependency it is bound to foster among adults who under other circumstances would have long moved beyond it, many of us were in those days expected to grow up instantly. What resulted was in many cases a mini-experience of adolescence, frequently pursued during summer school, and then a wholesale intellectual immersion into the concepts of adulthood with emotional integration, however, largely neglected. As a consequence, many religious even today are still working through independence issues while the vision of the clan has never been fully resolved. To complicate matters, our vocabulary now is "personal," holistic — in line with the workshops we attended and the books we read, but rarely has it been processed or integrated into the larger picture of life. Thus we have often merely the *appearance* of maturity. It is evident in all our documents, but because of the absence of a critical appropriation, it is also the reason so few of these documents truly move us. What we wrote has not "penetrated" many of us because our growth process was not adequately honored.

An example is the "reverse-oppression" and "tribal obsession" that can be found in the consensual model of decision making presently upheld as the clearest sign of our movement into more holistic ways of relating. Because the whole process of discernment and subsequent consensus appears to have been for many of us merely a "bandwagon value," espoused to honor the worth of each individual in the group but never adequately appropriated, the power of decision making has now, in many cases, passed over to the minority (sometimes even a minority of one) who holds out its objection when the rest of the assembly wishes to move on. The dissenters forever hold the floor and wear out the group until from sheer exhaustion the majority gives in and the few carry the day in the name of "reverence for the uniqueness of each person." The subtle return to clan behavior and its tyranny is noticed only by a small number who, if they object, are branded as "behind the times" while true reflection and discernment is aborted.

What we need perhaps more than anything else in this time of confusion is sincere and centered listening to the *words* we use and the *values* we espouse, as well as an honest appraisal of their validity. "Language," says Heidegger, "is the house of Being." Obedience to our documents and our policies may need to be, first and foremost, an honest acceptance of our brokenness in their regard and an effort to align *who we are* with *what we say.* Otherwise we not only fool ourselves but much more seriously we betray our call to individuation and condemn ourselves to remain stunted in our development.

Leadership here needs to trailblaze the questioning process. Few of us need many more documents and vision statements. What we need is to situate ourselves with respect to the ones we have and to allow ourselves to grow into their vision. Nor do I advocate the taking on of a great deal of guilt in this venture. None of our confusion is the result of intentional evil. It is, much rather, the consequence of growth adversely caught up in cultural and institutional paradigm shifts. To allow for some clarity and ultimately for some real communion in our vision we will have to allow ourselves some room for personal and in-depth reflection on the *meaning* of the values we proclaim.

There cannot be here any "right" or "wrong" answers either, for the vision we have is the vision that arises out of the level of consciousness on which we find ourselves, and, quite simply, we are not all in the same place. We will find, when we come to share our understandings, that we do not all agree, and we will need to let that be for a while. All of us will require the space and the peace to grow. Spiritual direction, counselling, therapy, and group support sessions will probably be very helpful here. We may discover that though we can share our perspectives, we cannot necessarily live together indiscriminately any more,[17] for our needs will reveal themselves as widely divergent and may need to be addressed in different settings. Intentional communities will have to be considered seriously, and some of us may need to live alone at least for some time.

In all of this the place of leadership will primarily have

to be that of co-discernment and challenge toward growth, and the place of chapters in the life of our congregations will have to be the same. If we are to work toward internalizing and appropriating the vision of our constitutions and our many mission statements over the last twenty-five years, our chapters might serve us best by offering us focused questions rather than acts and by inviting us to use these questions as a way of moving into depth both individually as well as together. In my moments of dreaming I envision a chapter whose message to the membership would quite simply acknowledge its own poverty and the destitution of our times:

> Sisters (Brothers), we gathered together during these weeks of Chapter to reflect on our call. At the end of our time together we have nothing to offer you except our own poverty and the trust that the Spirit of God who has wonderfully revealed this to us wills us to abide there for our own transformation and the transformation of the world. We ask you, therefore, to help us during these next six years to live into the following questions that have presented themselves to us over and over again during our deliberations; to abide in the waiting and thus to enable us all to become truly what God wants us to be. (This statement is then followed by reflective questions.)

In her address to the Leadership Conference of Women Religious in Spokane, Washington (August 23, 1990), Mary Jo Leddy speaks strongly in a similar vein when she calls leadership to "pursue the questions of the purpose and meaning of religious life in our culture." It is her view that "the exercise of leadership is significantly related to our choice of leading questions":

> My sense is that as long as we are led by the questions of WHAT and HOW and WHEN we will manage, we will cope, we will keep on keeping on. We will not feel a radical need for the Spirit of God or for one another. Once we begin to ask WHY, what is the point of this all, we will find ourselves — back to the wall, ear to the ground, every hair on our head counting on Love. And we may find ourselves becoming what we probably wanted to become when we first entered religious life — believers, women [men] of God.[18]

At this point it may be necessary to return again to our discussion concerning our levels of consciousness and the crises that befall us during times of transition, for I believe that the very structures of our institutions may make it difficult to have this dream of mine come true: to have us all abide in the questions and endure the pain of transformation.

— 3 —

RELATIONAL JUSTICE

Enduring the pain of communal and cultural transformation clearly requires a high degree of motivation and maturity (level III). As I have already suggested, however, it is unfortunately not at all certain that either of these are widely present among us. Functionalism (level II) in congregational structures is widespread, and among the membership, those who have successfully navigated the transcendence of clan values (level I) find themselves for the most part, and quite in line with the evolution of their consciousness, addressing independence issues (level II). Honoring the developmental process requires, therefore, a great deal of patience, and undue haste, regardless of the urgency of other concerns, will only further the relational drought in which so many of us already find ourselves.

No matter how pressing the demands of our mission both congregationally or individually, concentration on human interiority, hence on maturation and individuation, can simply no longer be sidestepped or ignored, for if it is not honored, it will inevitably destroy our broader efforts anyway. "Personal growth and social concerns are not mutually exclusive." In fact, "fundamental to social disorder is the disorder within each of us and . . . a re-ordering of society depends upon a re-ordering of individual lives."[19] The witness we hope to give professionally with respect to justice and the reign of God will only be as effective as the experience we have of it in the integrity of our own being, for *our very lives are the mission*. We bear within ourselves the death and the resurrection of the Christ, and the crises through which we are called to pass as we open up ever more authentically toward cosmic consciousness are the crucibles of our redemption, which ultimately effect the very Christification of the universe.

THE URGE TOWARD OBLIGATION

The preceding pages have highlighted that the disorder in our communal lives and its concomitant lack of justice need to be of serious concern to us. Here again we echo the culture in which we live. Psychiatrist Barbara R. Krasner, writing in *Foundations* now already over ten years ago, suggests that in Western society at large "relational poverty is currently unidentified, undefined, and unaddressed — much less redeemed. Yet relational poverty and the injustices on which it is built are the sources of unmitigated human suffering and chaos."[20] She identifies one of the sources of our culture's current epidemic of "relational poverty" as the dichotomy created in our society between two fundamental components of human relationship: (a) the impulse toward liberation, and (b) the impulse toward obligation. And she warns that if the complementary dynamics between these impulses are ignored relational injustice results.

Few of us can deny the emphasis on obligation our training provided for us in the past and the lack of deep inner freedom that was the result of our interminable "shoulds." Doing one's duty promptly and efficiently was ever the sign of a good religious. Self-lessness, at all times for the common good, was praised. In sickness and in health we dragged ourselves to our duty ever forgetful of ourselves. Agape meant losing oneself, pouring oneself out utterly, heedless of the self's own needs. The impulse toward obligation was alive and well among us. But what of the *self* we were giving up? Who was the *self* that we surrendered so willingly? What if the *self* of many religious had, for one reason or another, not emerged yet when we gave it up in the fervor of our vocation? What if it had been deadened, repressed, incarcerated? What if today we need *liberation*, if not an actual *birthing* of the *self* in order to respond truly and authentically to our communal obligations?

The need here may prove to be particularly acute among religious whose legitimate childhood dependency needs were never recognized and have as a consequence remained unfulfilled. We know today that the *self*-lessness, for example, that results when healthy narcissistic needs of infancy are not met can seriously endanger a person's capacity for authentic loving and mature relationships. It stifles a necessary sense of *self-worth*, of personal lovableness, and leads to adult narcissistic disorders that will drive one to seek forever and hopelessly the mother love and attention one was deprived of in early childhood. It goes without saying that this can work havoc in community.

A well-written and easily read little book by psychoanalyst Alice Miller, *Prisoners of Childhood*, compassionately explains what I am here describing. She sees this dilemma affecting many therapists.[21] But persons in helping professions generally might all do well to ponder its possibility in themselves. We frequently carry the virtues of our afflictions. The very sensitivity, therefore, with which we can be present to persons in need may have been learned in large measure in those childhood years when adjusting our needs to those of the adult world around us was the only way in which we could earn some of the affection we so desperately needed from our significant others. We quite literally may have adjusted our personality to fit the needs and desires of others. Thus we became convenient and responsible children in order to eke out what love we could to fulfill our own very legitimate needs. In Jungian terms one might say that we donned the "helper" persona and that we have been connected to it ever since. We spend our lives seeking to be of service, being sensitively present to others, empowering them, working toward their healing. The persona patterns of our ministry and our interpersonal behavior, however, speak of the violence done to our childhood needs.

Now, whereas our gifts may in a strange way be the glory of our wounds and speak to the grace of God and the resilience of the human spirit, the wounds out of which they grew will nevertheless need to be acknowledged lest they begin to fester and destroy our relationships. What are our regular patterns of relating? Do we truly love each other in our differences, for example, or do we merely seek each other out and lift each other up to fulfill our needs? Do we sincerely love ourselves? How many of us, because of the relational poverty of our childhood do not even know what authentic love of self means? These are important questions that cry for answers if we are to liberate ourselves from the impulse toward obligation that has dominated our lives so long under the guise of virtue and has reduced us relationally to such destitution.

A therapist friend of mine not long ago made this sad comment about our life together: "Religious are experts at observing the 'Greatest Commandment,'" she noted. "They love their neighbor *exactly* as they love themselves. There is, therefore, very little love to go around." As shocking as this observation is, we need to give it an honest hearing. Poverty is a disgrace only when it is culpable. For us, much of what Krasner refers to as the relational poverty that remains unidentified and, therefore, unaddressed can be redeemed only when we allow ourselves to *face* the taboo regions of our childhood and give way to legitimate grief, when we can let ourselves mourn what never was and therefore never will be, when we can work through the arduous task of learning to accept that all of this may not be anybody's fault[22] and at the same time permit ourselves to experience the anger at the unfairness of it all, when we can gently start seeing our worth independent of our "obligations-fulfilled," when we can begin to love ourselves.

In my teaching on this subject[23] I often refer to Rollo May's references to the Orestes myth[24] and suggest that (at some time on one's journey into honesty) one needs to "kill" one's mother so that she might finally be able to become one's friend. By this is meant that unless we face and then "kill" our childhood dependencies, in whatever disguise they may appear in our present situation, we will never be able to relate on adult terms. If our "mother" continues to haunt us, we will find it very difficult, if not impossible, to see the persons we live with in their own right and to transcend the symbiosis that fruitlessly enchains us and destroys all other relationships as well as the communities in which we live.

In the trial of Orestes, "the tremendous issue [that had] to be decided [was] whether a person is to be judged guilty for killing a dominating and exploitative parent. Since the outcome [was] in actuality . . . crucial for the future of [humankind], the gods from Olympus [came] down to participate in the debate." Orestes was saved by Athena's vote in his favor. The theme here was the killing of one's mother, but the meaning revolved around "the struggle of Orestes, the son, *for his existence as a person.*"[25]

The urgency for liberation among some religious may appear extreme to others for whom this issue never seemed major, or who have not yet become aware that it even exists. Its extremity, however, is proportional only to the extremity of "obligation" experienced previously. Unless we raise it to consciousness and deal with it, we are the victims of our past; it "has" us, instead of our having it. Very often the "formation" we received upon entering religious life quite unconsciously fed into our childhood dependencies and the excessive sense of obligation and guilt accompanying them. This exacerbated the problem for many of us. We ought not rule out, moreover, the painful possibility that the motivations for our "vocation" may have been derived there as well. All of this can be extremely difficult to acknowledge and work through, but we need to remember that none of it is bad. It is merely a sign of our widespread woundedness and is not irreparable. It is dangerous and destructive only to the extent to which it is ignored or denied and thus leads to destructive and unjust behavior on our part.

THE NEED FOR LIBERATION

Much of what we have been discussing in the last several pages revolves around our movement from clan needs to independence. The myths of old attributed such a journey to the heros, for the ancients were keenly aware of the courage and perseverance it required. It would be a mistake to assume that the situation is any different today. The present cultural crisis calls for heros as well and needs the contemporary religious to be among them.

Adult lives of dependency lead to repression of the queries necessary to rework the imprint of injustice that our past patterns of communal behavior left with us.[26] Adult independence, on the other hand, though ideally this is a matter for late adolescence and the emergence of identity, opens the way to taking ownership of one's life (liberation) and to responding ultimately beyond the group's "should" to an ever-wider world of obligations. This, however, requires courage. What the religious engaged on this journey needs above all else from her community, therefore, is sensitivity, honesty, and the avoidance of a severe, judgmental attitude.

We have already discussed that circumvention, as desirable as it may appear, is not possible in our movement through the levels of maturation. Although the necessary passage through any particular level may be accelerated for an older person, none of the levels of consciousness can be skipped. By the same token, unnecessary prolongation of one's stay on any level of awareness is equally problematic and can only lead to stultification and fixation of growth. In all of this it is ever helpful to keep in mind that, as necessary as it is to honor the need for independence within the context of community, our communal goal (and also the goal of all of humankind in its maturation process) ultimately is holistic interdependence. Our patient and loving being together in the meantime can, however, truly be a difficult and painful business. This is largely because identity is achieved at least initially through separation and exclusion rather than through the inclusion that is so often seen as the lifeblood of community. The separation discussed here is, perhaps, best understood as a process of consciousness fittingly called "nihilation" (Sartre), for it fosters ego development by means of distancing — at the expense, therefore, of intimacy and closeness.

In early child development, the child's movement "away from" his or her significant other is motivated by the need to take hold of himself or herself: One finds the "I" *that one is* by discovering that one *is not the other* and experimenting with that discovery. Thus one reinforces the "I" that one is by intentional opposition to the "not-I." In this way one's individuality gets strengthened. Though self-assertion may initially be exciting and even playful for the child, it rarely is a pleasant experience for the parents, for it generally appears as willfulness and can easily disrupt an otherwise peaceful household. Not much is different when this experience befalls us in our adult years. Nihilation frequently announces itself by a more pronounced need to withdraw, an unwilling-ness to be present, and an ever-intensifying desire to make one's own choices one's own way. It often will show itself in competitiveness and the drive to be better than, smarter than, more recognized than others. It feels charged by an obsession with winning, with being in control. There is a general feeling of "over-againstness," a need to strike out on one's own. Among religious, nihilation may, furthermore, be intensified as a reaction to what they perceive, rightly or wrongly, as the still prevailing "clan" mentality of the past. Here the possibility of harmful exaggeration and consequent distortion is particularly strong. If one is not careful, one can therefore quite readily become as oppressive as the system one is criticizing and even do so in the name of freedom and progress — with total blindness and best intentions.

One of the obvious risks for religious congregations whose members find themselves in the throes of identity concerns is that when the need for independence is experi-enced by some religious, they may wish to move away from the group permanently. Painful as this may be, these are risks that nevertheless must be taken. To block the process through general rules and prohibitions because of the possi-ble difficulties that may be encountered by some would be a betrayal of our call to wholeness and of the necessary re-spect for individual differences that this process requires. In the final analysis, however, and hard as this may sound, it is again important to remind ourselves that total independence is not what we have committed ourselves to. Here the gentle presence of empowering leadership can be of great help in giving time and space while at the same time co-discerning the movement of the Spirit.

The *why* behind the contemporary phenomenon of religious women or men living alone cannot, of course, be reduced to independence issues. There are, as we know, many reasons why single living is seemingly becoming a lifestyle among us. For a growing number of us, some of these result from ministry commitments and from the absence of other religious in the *diaspora* in which we find ourselves. There is also the increasing problem of emotional fatigue and of our apparent inability at this time to address this communally. Then there are those among us who find it difficult, perhaps even impossible, to live relationally, whose entrance into community before the reforms of Vatican II was not based on this requirement[27] and who now need to be invited to live alone both for their own peace of mind, as well as that of the other community members. Whatever our communal and individual reasons with respect to living arrangements may be, however, a *conscious* acceptance of them on our part is most important. If, as we claim, religious life is in transition, then the more aware of it we are, the freer we are in it. Aimless drifting into diverse lifestyles is not responsible adult behavior and speaks of the clan's enslavement to fate. What we become will have to be our choice, for it will, whether we like to admit it or not, be our responsibility.

The more advanced stages of individualization and functionalism, as the second level of consciousness has been identified in chapter 1, will see a preoccupation with rational ideals, with abstraction, objectification, organization, clarity, and calculation. As religious working through this phase we may find ourselves speaking long and passionately about the ideals of religious life and wanting to "organize" the community we live in accordingly. At the same time we will place great emphasis on our profession, on education, training, and expertise, on career advancement. With respect to the larger congregational picture, our concerns with government plans and policies, Robert's Rules, the proper observance of the rules of subsidiarity, absolute consensus in decision making, measurable criteria for living simplicity of life, for setting community goals, for evaluating our newer members — all can become major issues for us during our sojourn on this level of awareness. By them we judge the relevance of religious life. Our energy is spent in drawing up decrees. Our worth as religious, our value as members in our province, our unit, our region, perhaps the entire institute, and frequently even our potential for leadership is measured there.

The frustration level accompanying such concerns, especially as one after the other they prove disappointing to us, can be intense. Initially it may, therefore, get displaced as we look outside ourselves for every possible reason things are not working. Of course, the fact that many of our congregational priorities are still centered in the realm of functionality may also delay our disillusionment. We can lull ourselves into believing that this is what our life together is all about. We can even successfully advance ourselves in such a life — play, for example, the "Sister Mary Corporate" role as one of the newer members of my acquaintance facetiously calls those women in her congregation whom she sees as caught up in their hospital system. And we can even feel good about our achievements. Sooner or later, however, we will experience the tastelessness of it all and our drive toward wholeness and depth will again claim us.

As I mentioned in chapter 1, it is my sense that functionality generally is beginning to loosen its grip on our culture, that the values it professes are beginning to be viewed more critically, and that humankind as a whole is in crisis toward a deeper vision. The signs of new life are still in many respects embryonic, of course, and often this new life gets smothered again by the will to power and the consumerism of our age. But the days of commodity rule and functionalism, of objectification and rationalism are numbered. Their demise rests in their own ineffectiveness to deal with the social concerns of our time and in the growing awareness by all of us that this is so.

Again, what is true for our culture also applies to us. The overall disenchantment felt by so many of us with our own life priorities, with what appears to be an excessive corporate concern for finance by many of our congregations, with structural preoccupations, with the incessant drawing up of policies and objectives, all speak to the decline of functionality among us as well. As such, I hold, it is a sign of the Spirit. "What gives me hope," says Mary Jo Leddy, "is that the loss of meaning in religious life is being increasingly felt as a painful reality. There would be little hope if we had all adjusted to this situation and accepted it as normal."[28] In spite of our seemingly endless problems and apparent hopelessness, something within us is alive and well, waiting patiently and moving us persistently toward our own liberation.

— 4 —

THE LOVE OF CHRIST
IMPELS US

Not long ago during a congregational planning session I had the privilege of finding myself in a small reflection group with one of our province's still very active senior sisters. She shared with us how for many years she had struggled with negativity arising from expectations related to community life. Few of the sisters, she noted, were ever at home when the community gathered regularly for prayer. None of the old "togetherness" was left. Schedules were extremely diverse, and everyone seemed so tired and worn out. She found herself growing disenchanted, disgruntled even, bordering on the judgmental. Then one morning, she told us, everything changed for her. She had been reading Paul's second letter to the Corinthians and stopped short at the passage: *"The love of Christ impels us who have reached the conviction that since one died for all, all died. He died for all so that those who live might* live no longer for themselves, but for him who for their sakes died and was raised up. *Because of this we no longer look on anyone in terms of mere human judgment"* (2 Cor. 5:14–16). She kept repeating: "The love of Christ impels us." Somehow this insight had changed her life. She knew now deep within herself that there was no one in her community who was not somehow "impelled" by the love of Christ. "We see our service differently," she said. "Our community needs are diverse; consequently our expectations vary, but 'the love of Christ impels us,' and, therefore, we are one."

I was amazed at the releasement with which she shared her insight, at her ability during our discussions to "let go" and "let be," at the serenity that seemed to have reached her deepest center. Her disposition brought back to me what months earlier I had "dreamed about" in *Living the Vision:*

> I seriously doubt that community is fostered primarily by what we do in it or about it: with how many persons we live, how often we meet, what we meet about, and whether there is or is not an agenda for the meeting. Although these issues are important, our main concern, simplistic as this may sound, is in the last analysis *whether we trust one another;* whether we can be vulnerable, poor, in each other's presence; whether there is, when we encounter one another, a basic stance of openness to the self-revelation of God in this meeting.[29]

"The love of Christ impels us.... We no longer look on anyone in terms of mere human judgment." Perhaps our transformation into interdependence and authentic communion holds within it the insight of this passage. Judgment and the law belong primarily to functional categories. Although they are useful there and will continue also to play their role in the necessary day-to-day transactions of our life, the love of Christ moves them off center stage. For us to hear the whisperings of interdependence and of authentic communion we will need to be *impelled* by the Christ.

A CALL TO CONVERSION

Something radically new, just like something deeply personal, is difficult to write about. The concepts are usually not available yet to contain it and it is, therefore, open to misunderstanding. Much of it is also still in the process of emerging, of birthing itself. Some of it may not even be there yet although its presence is mysteriously felt because it somehow announces itself in its absence — in the longing, the felt lack, the emptiness. One can best speak of the new or the radical in stories, in analogies. One can live into it, but it is almost useless to write about it. The written word tends to encapsule, to finalize, to take on an authority it does not have. Somehow in the public eye the writer is also not permitted to change his or her mind without appearing shallow. This can stifle her or his creative flow and imposes a burden neither deserved nor warranted.

I suspect that one of the reasons so many of humankind's truly creative visionaries never wrote can be found in the very creativity with which they spoke. They were in labor with it. It was groaning within them, flowing through them, and would stand for no closure. Jesus never wrote, nor did he ever order that his thoughts be written down, finalized, dogmatized. His radically new vision was also deeply personal — vibrant, alive, in flux. It emerged from experience and invited it. It spoke of risk, of putting one's hand to the plow and never looking back, of a doing that flowed from being, not from speculating. To write his vision down would have been to imprison it somehow and to distance it, in a way, from the Body that was called to live it.

We are that Body. For it to live is for us to move with the creative flow of Christ's vision. Nothing that is written in these pages, therefore, about interdependent, interpersonal living, about "participatory consciousness," as Bruteau calls the vision of level III,[30] can be accepted as final. As was mentioned already, it is not intended to be that, for closure would destroy the emergence and foreclose on the grace that is dawning in each of us and for our *living*. If we believe Paul's letter to the Corinthians and accept that "since one died for all, all died," then we will also have to accept that in his life all live and that, since he rose, we too shall rise with him. We live in the fullness of time and bear within us the death and the resurrection of the Christ. Our lives give witness to this as the universe is groaning within our very being waiting for its fulfillment in Christ.

This is not just pious phraseology. It addresses us in the very marrow of our existence. That is *why* we are experiencing the anguish of meaninglessness; that is *why* we are held in crisis today. The transformation of consciousness to which we find ourselves compelled at this moment in our history is part of a momentous Christification process. Paul meant it when he suggested that in our very own flesh we "fill up what is lacking in the sufferings of Christ for the sake of his body, the church" (Col. 1:24). As I see it, ours is the task of personalizing once again what has been written about Jesus, of enfleshing the Gospel, of living the Incarnation. Much of what empowered the early Christian community has suffered the calcification of time[31] and needs to regain its passion. Although by our baptism we are with all other Christians grafted into this passion, as religious we covenant ourselves to it specifically by means of the vows we live out in community.

Now none of this is really understandable or even of much significance on the functional level of existence. What, after all, does "enfleshing the Gospel" and "Christifying the cosmos" really mean? How can it be figured out? Where is it explained? How can it be organized, objectified, systematized, dogmatized? On the clan level, too, it makes little sense, since the personal freedom and struggle it requires are foreign to the clan where things are done all together, blindly, where all questioning, let alone depth questing, is seen as inappropriate if not sinful, and where the predigested is the status quo.

We need a new mode of consciousness, therefore, in order for us truly to understand and appreciate the message of 2 Corinthians 5:14–16. We need a genuine "gestalt shift," as Bruteau calls it, "in the whole way of seeing our relations to one another," to ourselves also, and to God, so that "our behavior patterns are reformed from the inside out" and our disposition is fundamentally altered. We need a "revolution of consciousness."[32]

REVOLUTION NOT REBELLION

It is important for us to note that Bruteau distinguishes what she calls "revolution" from what is normally understood as "rebellion." The latter, she says, is not total enough because it lacks sufficient consciousness. In it one experiences the mere shuffling of positions, the replacement of one set of rules by another, while the structure remains basically the same. A rebellion effects no fundamental change, no depth conversion. If there has been oppression before, there will be oppression after. There is merely a transfer of power from one person to another or from one person to a group. For our purposes, much of what I discussed in chapter 2 under the heading "Subtle Dependency Patterns," illustrates this position quite readily. There I suggested that a change of vocabulary can neatly cover up superficiality but leave unaddressed fundamental patterns of seeing and behaving (in chapter 2 it was a pattern of control). We think, therefore, that change has been effected, while in reality there has been only a rearrangement of power.

A revolution of consciousness, on the other hand, calls for transformation *at the very root of our existence.* It calls for a regrounding of beliefs, a breakthrough of new meaning. Because for most of us this breakthrough seems still in its advent, a description of how the vision it shall offer will affect community life may be somewhat premature and can at best be sketchy. Although what community life ought no longer to be can be surmised from our discussion of the functional and clan levels of consciousness in the previous chapters, what we may hope for in the future is less clear and can, at best, be approached only tentatively. A reflection on certain

THE LOVE OF CHRIST IMPELS US

key shifts in our fundamental modes of behavior, as I identified them several years ago in *Releasement*,[33] may, however, be helpful here.

First, there will have to be a deliberate movement from over-againstness to mutual affirmation. We will remember that the third level of consciousness can break through only when ego-enhancement and independence have climaxed in the experience of the total futility of "external props" and when one is thus opened to the possibility of interiority. "The perspective that arises out of a confrontational attitude is obsessed with self-preservation and enhancement."[34] The other is ever seen as a threat to this. When, however, my identity needs have been adequately recognized and worked through and I have finally resigned myself to the fact that I do not need to shine on someone else's (or even a self-imposed) scale of comparative excellence in order to be accepted, successful, and even lovable, I can move on. Thus I am freed for more authentic intimacy and with it mutual affirmation becomes not only a possibility, but even a conscious desire, a goal. I begin to find my heart, as it were, through the service of others in an exchange of creative energy that does not deny the other in his or her uniqueness but rather out of that uniqueness embraces him or her.

Again Bruteau's magnificent description of participatory consciousness cited first in *Living the Vision* comes to mind:

> When I love with participatory consciousness, I see that what the other *is* is some of my life-energy living there, and what I am is some of the other's life-energy living here in me. I can no longer divide the world into "we's" and "they's." ... In some way, my boundary has

become less definite in the sense of being less hard and sealed off. My selfhood has become radiant, streaming out from me, and is found participating in the other even as it is found in me.[35]

There is in participatory consciousness no room for envy, since we can finally see that one powerful life energy flows through all of us and that therefore the other's gift graces not only her or him, but all of us as well. This must not be mistaken as a simplistic return to clan absorption. It shows, rather, a conscious integration of all previous levels of consciousness into a unified whole. Thus the individual person is clearly respected:

Creative love is entirely the protection and nurturance of personal freedom and uniqueness. It is precisely because a person as a whole is absolutely unique that it transcends all the categories by which abstractive consciousness would classify it. The single large life in which I participate is a *community of whole unique selves who freely form and constitute this large unifying life by the intercommunication of their creative love energies.*[36]

The believing heart sees this love energy as God energy, and the softening of the boundaries as the breakthrough of God where, as Eckhart would have us understand, all things, all persons, become the manifestation of the divine and where opposition, over-againstness, and ultimately war simply become impossible. For if I truly see with this vision, how can I possibly allow the God in me to hate the God in you?

Compassion is the outflow of such a vision: I share the other's gifts as well as her or his wounds and brokenness — not just the brokenness inflicted by an unjust world from which I will try to liberate the oppressed (external compassion). I also share the brokenness that brings me home to myself and thus has me stand in solidarity with my sisters and brothers in their personal pain and sin — experiencing the at-oneness that knows of the collective evil and responsibility of humankind, that feels in its very core that "there go I ..." (internal compassion).

The consciousness here described is existential, experiential rather than speculative: perceiving persons according to preconceived definitions — in their essences — sorting out their attributes for the purpose of categorizing. It encounters others from the inside, enters into their lives, not merely with gut instinct, but through a more refined at-oneness perhaps best described as intellectual intuition where feeling is integrated with reason (level I with level II) and thus moves naturally to insight. Paul's observation that "the life I live now is not my own; Christ is living in me (Gal. 2:20), might serve as a good example of this existential at-oneness. He certainly did not imply absorption, symbiotic union, when he made this statement. He, Paul, was and remained very much Paul. Yet, somehow, he experienced Christ from the inside, inextricably united even in profound otherness. In existential insight I too know from my very depths that the life I live now is no longer my own but that the other, the world, God lives in me. My entire perceptive framework changes accordingly and with it my modes of behavior.

In religious life we call the creative love described here our covenant with one another. The above is its visionary possibility. What it would do for our community living would indeed be transformative! For the present it is a rare phenomenon, but I do not think it is impossible for any of us. The vision is ours for the openness, the willing availability, the patient endurance, the humble surrender. It will require, furthermore, a tender self-possession on the part of all of us, for only those who possess themselves can give themselves up without betraying themselves and losing their inner core. It will require releasement — that gentle abandon that can let go of all pre-judgments, presuppositions, assumptions, and undue expectations, that can let the other be, can empower, and rejoice in God's creative outpouring.

The second shift mentioned in *Releasement* is clearly already subsumed under the first: "From domination and mandatory conformity we embrace the relational: we honor diversity even as we uphold community."[37] We have here a clear integration of level I with participatory consciousness, which absolves us from the guilt so frequently experienced because of our differences and invites us to celebrate them instead. Much can be learned from this for community life: The concern, for example, with minority vocations (or perhaps more accurately stated, the concern about their absence) in so many communities particularly in the United States could quite easily be eliminated if we would allow ourselves to address our seeming inability truly to celebrate diversity. Our inadequacy in this respect is particularly noticeable when minority differences are clearly visible, such as in racial diversity. But it also exists for other ethnic variations. Cultural behavior patterns and habits, ethnic pride, aesthetic preferences, family values can differ greatly within races as well as among races. They can be very subtle and need to be treated with great sensitivity. It is not a complement to tell someone that he or she is beginning to be "just like us." The melting pot, at best, is an illusion, at worst, a violation. Our at-oneness will not be fostered by absorption into the majority's standards. It grows, paradoxically, in the creative letting be, in the honoring and the celebration of uniqueness. When minority members can sense a sincere welcome of their entirety — values, language, behavior, accent, food, and all — they will experience communion, and the problem of their low numbers among us will, I believe, be notably reduced.

In *Living the Vision* I have addressed at length the obvious diversity now present among our newer members. It goes without saying that participatory consciousness will significantly affect the way we look at our welcoming policies in their regard as well. Not only will we no longer feel the need to supply them with all the decisions and answers for their lives, since many of them enter at a mature age, have dealt with life's questions when they arose, and are quite capable of continuing to do so now, but we will in fact want *to share our own poverty with them,* walk with them in mutuality, in co-discernment, in friendship. We will resist putting any of them into predetermined categories (according to age, professional training, ethnicity, etc.), and we will want to celebrate them in their diversity and in their unique giftedness for community and mission.

The third shift to be expected as participatory consciousness graces us is the obvious one from independence to interdependence. In our age and culture it addresses itself particularly to individualism — an excessive preoccupation with our own private concerns and needs — and opens us to the cosmic. I have heard much in the last several years, both in my own congregation as well as in others, about the dangers of individualism among religious. I am sure it exists, since the age we live in is infested with it. I am not sure, however, that when we talk about its presence among us we are always addressing the same issue, nor am I convinced that what we seem to fear is in fact always a "danger." Might our concern not center at least sometimes around the legitimate issues discussed in chapter 3: our ontological need to experience independence in order to open up for ourselves the possibility of interdependence? This need clearly puts some of our accepted and sanctioned communal behavior patterns at risk, but it cannot, therefore, be avoided or condemned. Our congregational survival depends on our addressing it and allowing it ultimately to grow into authentic mutuality.

Our culture's influence of selfishness and of "looking out for number one" is undoubtedly a force to be reckoned with, and sincere discernment by each of us individually is certainly necessary here. Our collective behavior patterns, however, need to be examined as well. Here "doing our own thing" for purposes of advancement, financial benefits, status of one kind or another, can be a much more subtle form of individualism with dire consequences for the survival of our founding charism and the vision of cosmic responsibility to which we are called. The resistance to losing corporate power and functional significance all in the name of congregational security may be imprisoning us on the highest levels of functionality without our even being aware of it. Whenever corporateness prevents us from giving priority to congregational works of mercy, collective individualism "has" us, whether we want to admit it or not, and no amount of "piety in print" will save us in such situations from the arduous responsibility of examining our priorities lest our vision fixate and we betray the mandate of our founding. The movement from independence and success to interdependence and mutuality is one of surrender, of letting go, of finding strength in weakness, of vulnerability. This is by no means easy for anyone. It may be even harder for a group.

There is an open-endedness to one's life when one encounters oneself and others as *persons* rather than mere functionaries. There is risk, wonder, and mystery. One moves away from abstractions into the realm of the concrete, the experiential. Clearly defined objectives are not as important as they used to be, nor are predictability and closure. All this can be risky and uncomfortable for anyone who still sees efficiency as the crown of ministry and service. It helps, therefore, to remember how messy and, in many respects, unorganized as well as unpredictable Jesus' life was, so that we can let go of our excessive need to be in control of our lives and of one another.

We really *have no control*, of course, of the *truly* important aspect of our lives: Maturation, insight, compassion, friendship, understanding, genuine kindness and tenderness, releasement, and true freedom are all gifts, and so are our growth pains, the depth crises of our lives that will lead us to surrender our power, and so is decline, and so is death. To stock our barns with personal or congregational predictabilities, therefore, is foolishness (Luke 12:18–19). I do not wish to imply here that intelligent planning and foresight are not necessary in our lives. I am merely suggesting that personal or participatory consciousness has us shift priorities. This will happen gently, without much fanfare or the need to make major pronouncements. The crisis we find ourselves in today is readying us for this grace, but we can also deny ourselves this possibility; herein lies the danger.

We need to remember that the revolutionary consciousness that beckons us out of our present-day crisis and into cosmic compassion and love is new only in its originality for our time. In a very real sense Heidegger's observation that the future comes toward us out of the past holds true here, for participatory consciousness is really nothing other than Christ consciousness. Our movement into it is ever our baptismal response to the Gospel. It is a retrieval of our heritage, an appropriation of the ancient wisdom of our tradition, and a seeing with the new eyes of those who have grown into its vision for the transformation of the world.

As the 1989 joint assembly put it: "Religious in the year 2010 will serve a prophetic role in the church and society." They will live a spirituality of wholeness fostering: "(a) participation and harmony among all people, (b) healthy personal and interpersonal relationships, (c) reverences for the earth, (d) integration of spirituality and technology on behalf of the gospel." Their communities "will be characterized by inclusivity. . . . "

This is our covenant, for we are impelled toward it by the love of Christ who "died for all so that those who live might live no longer for themselves but for him who for their sakes died and was raised up."

— Conclusion —
SOME THOUGHTS FOR THE NOW

"SNIFFING-OUT" TIME

Among the Gospel accounts of the call to discipleship the story told by John has always intrigued me. It is different from the other three highly action-oriented stories, which invite us to become fishers not of fish but of all people. Somehow I find it gentler in tone. It allows the disciples some time to get to know Jesus, to find out more about him. It gives them what I have come to call "some sniffing-out" time: " 'Rabbi, ... where do you stay?' 'Come and see,' he answered. So they went to see where he was lodged, and stayed with him that day" (John 1:38–39).

A friend of mine who is very fond of and gifted with animals, especially those of the "stray" kind, told me one time that all one needs to do to befriend an animal is to allow it some time to sniff one out. "Just be very nonassuming," she said. "Be about your business and give the animal the time it needs to get used to its surroundings and then to get used to you. Pretty soon if you do not fuss with it, but are gentle in its

83

presence, it will come around and then you can befriend it."
It is my sense that humans are really not very different from
animals: We need time to "sniff each other out." Perhaps this
is something that we forget at times in our living together.

Although intentional communities will, I believe and
pray, soon become the norm,[38] there is, at present, really
very little stability in our living groups. This makes it doubly important that our expectation for instantly meaningful
interrelationships be realistically checked. We cannot forget
that every moving in, as well as every moving out, renders
the community we live in a new one. Each new community
will once again need time to adjust to itself. Human beings
are more than functionaries or pieces in a puzzle. We are *persons.* This means that each of us has his or her unique fears,
hopes, needs for privacy, and needs for togetherness. We
cannot assume that anyone's requirements or desires will
speak to all of us; we cannot even assume that we know what
the other person's requirements or desires are. We need time
to get to know each other, we need to know and accept that
we need that time, and we need that time in an unthreatening
environment.

The implications of this may surprise some of us. They
may even upset us at first, especially if we are used to
very structured and congregationally approved schedules for
community interaction. Two examples come to mind: First,
it may not be possible for a new group to engage realistically in high-level goal setting at the beginning of the year
or whenever they first come together. This is especially so if
later on they will be held accountable for these goals. Since
even such obvious givens as a common language may turn
out to be anything but clear as we live together and slowly —

sometimes painfully — find out that what one person meant was not what another person understood, it may be wise to limit initial meetings of the group to the bare essentials of living space maintenance and leave deeper philosophical commitments for much later. "Time together" commitments, for example, may be very difficult to schedule in a new group. Very realistically, we may need to find out first how deeply we desire to be together, what our recreational and inspirational preferences are, *who we are* that commit ourselves to be together. Furthermore, if we have not lived together, none of us are used to each other's ministry involvements. Often we tend to judge the availability of others by our own and can then easily feel "neglected" or not cared about when others are not able to be with us during our free time. To make serious plans about these issues may, therefore, simply be unrealistic until we have "sniffed" each other out.

The second example concerns our need and at times our "shoulds" about praying together. If the realistic commitment to common values happens only slowly, so does faith sharing and meaningful prayer. Whereas it is true that anyone can put a prayer service together (many of us have collected samples of these for every imaginable occasion and can whip up a candle and a shell or flower in no time to provide the proper "holy space"), it is not at all a foregone conclusion that we can all *pray* together. Oh, we can recite psalms together, sing hymns together, and even "share" together, but there is sharing, and then there is *sharing.* Though we can all utter profundities, keeping one another "out" has been developed by most of us to a fine art and we can even be sincere in all of this. Faith sharing requires trust; it requires "sniffing-out time," regardless of our congregational at-oneness and "common" charism. Perhaps initially our sharing should only be minimal, if at all — a prayer of petition, perhaps. Gradually, as our trust grows (and that will vary with each person and may never happen with some), more depth can emerge. We are like blossoms. We open with the warmth of the sun.

The story of the befriending of the fox in Antoine de Saint Exupery's *The Little Prince* is a helpful reminder for all new communities, no matter how often they get formed in a single house and even in a single year:

The fox gazed at the little prince, for a long time.

"Please — tame me!" he said.

"I want to, very much," the little prince replied. *"But I have not much time.* I have friends to discover, and a great many things to understand."

"One only understands the things that one tames," said the fox. "[People] *have no more time to understand anything.* They buy things all ready made at the shops. But there is no shop anywhere where one can buy friendship, and so [people] have no friends any more. *If you want a friend, tame me..."*

"What must I do, to tame you?" asked the little prince.

"You must be very patient," replied the fox. "First you will sit down at a little distance from me — like that — in the grass. I shall look at you out of the corner of my eye, and you will say nothing. *Words are the source of misunderstandings.* But you will sit a little closer to me, every day..."

The next day the little prince came back.

"It would have been better to come back at the same hour," said the fox. "If, for example, you come at four o'clock in the afternoon, then at three o'clock I shall begin to be happy. I shall feel happier and happier as the hour advances. At four o'clock, I shall already be worrying and jumping about. I shall show you how happy I am! But if you come at just any time, I shall never know at what hour my heart is to be ready to greet you ... *One must observe the proper rites ..."*

"What is a rite?" asked the little prince.

"Those also are actions too often neglected," said the fox.[39]

The needs that many of us have and the living situations in which we find ourselves at present often are at odds. Perhaps we need a little compassion for one another: put aside all negative presuppositions, assume that all of us are doing our best, show kindness, so that we can "blossom forth" in each other's presence with the appropriate "rites" for our situation.

STABILITY AND SPACE

Lately I have wondered whether perhaps the American frontier mentality of space to conquer and places to see, mixed with a special brand of the biblical "pilgrim people" concept, does not in a subtle way have all of us believing that the only way to be about what is truly significant is to live with one foot in and one foot out of our community homes, to be detached enough to move wherever we must at a moment's notice. We are today truly busy about many things. Often we call our business "ministry," and almost always it takes precedence over any other concern in our life.

Much can be and has been said about the values of detachment, and I do not wish to question the good that has been done because we were free to pick up and leave all at a moment's notice. What does need to be observed, however, is (a) that a high degree of energy is required for such mobility, an energy that belongs to youth and health, and (b) that many of us presently still in the mainstream of ministry in our congregations have neither. We are, whether we like it or not, an aging group with the legitimate needs that go with aging. To deny this is simply to be unrealistic and to impose guilt where guilt ought not to be felt.

There is a sensitive balance between being about the *mission beyond one's gates* and being about the *mission within*. Congregationally, we have always spent a great amount of our energy with the former. The second half of life in which the majority of us find ourselves at this time in our history, however (and, surprisingly, in which a large number of the newer members seeking entrance into our communities find themselves as well), mandates that we concern ourselves also with the latter. Sadly enough, this mandate does not always get a sympathetic hearing among us. One is accused of advocating "navel gazing," of wanting to create "therapeutic communities" at the expense of the mission. What is ignored or perhaps not recognized in such accusations, however, is that being about the *mission within* is a necessary prerequisite for being a "pilgrim people," that the *mission beyond one's gates* does not happen unless we address concerns for our personal development and growth.

It is almost as if the energy focus shifts during maturation. Whereas during our youth much of our ministry was also connected with our identity and therefore had a natural outward focus, the energy of our maturing years centers around depth intimacy, generativity, and wisdom. If it is not honored there, it quite naturally depletes and we find ourselves deprived not only interiorly but exteriorly as well. The high level of fatigue among religious today speaks for itself. As we discussed at length throughout this book, the crisis of our culture and, by extension, the crisis in our midst is due largely to the climax in functionalism and its felt inadequacy among many. The cry today is for depth; this *is* the place of mission for us at this time.

One of the major ways in which community life can help further this mission is to provide us with the opportunity for stability and space. "Sniffing each other out," as we have already indicated, requires a great deal of time. It becomes near to impossible when local communities turn into grand central stations. Only time will provide the chance for the shedding of personas, the lowering of defenses, the nurturing of friendships, and the building of a home. Only time given to adult togetherness will provide the safety for working out differences and for learning to communicate. We need the patience as well as the generosity for "taming" one another and ourselves. If we move every time things get difficult, neither we nor the community with whom we have committed ourselves to growth will be able to develop. We will not be able to experience true intimacy and generativity either, for both demand a high degree of personal integrity and development if they are not to degenerate into the sentimental.

A second high priority for the mission of interiority is space. Again this may sound like a selfish requirement, but it is a known fact that even animals have territorial needs and will attack when their instincts are violated. Humans are no different. The violence in our overcrowded cities can at least partially be attributed to the space deprivation experienced there. Religious, too, have space needs. These may not have been evident as much when we had almost no personal belongings or diverse professional requirements and when conversation and personal interrelationships were kept at a minimum among us, but they are becoming ever more noticeable today. Nor is it helpful to respond to our times with homilies about the "good old days when we were really poor and kept silence." Our reality has changed. Our professions in many instances make legitimate demands for computers, books, clothes, etc., and although honest discernment with regard to simplicity of life is ever necessary, the little convent cubicles clearly will not do any longer to contain us.

Put quite simply: Adult bodies need adult space, and adult psyches do as well. To it we can withdraw at the appropriate time to find the solitude we legitimately and often desperately require so that later on we can return refreshed and give ourselves with renewed strength to the building of a healthy and a wholesome community. What exactly these observations will mean for us in terms of our choice of living arrangements will need to be worked out by each community and individual member in that community. I wish here simply to give voice to an important concern and thus help further discussion of this topic and minimize guilt.

IT HAS EVERYTHING TO DO
WITH KINDNESS

The story is told of three Chicago businessmen who one evening were particularly in a rush to catch their train home. As they were hurrying through the ticket gate, one of them pushed a young boy who was selling apples from a movable stand. The stand toppled and the apples came tumbling to the floor. Two of the men rushed on to connect with their train, but the third noticed that the young boy was blind. With one desperate parting glance in the direction of his transportation he stopped to pick up the apples for the youngster. The boy thanked him and then, as he was leaving asked him: "Mister, are you Jesus?" I remember not long ago telling this story, the source of which I can no longer remember, to one of my friends who had had a particularly rough time of it in community in the last several years. She filled up with tears as she heard it: "That's it," she said, "isn't it? It has everything to do with kindness."

What if we would let a little kindness into our gatherings? I have often wondered what community meetings would look like then. So often they become the projection centers of our unaddressed issues as we evaluate each other and the group in terms of our voiced and unvoiced expectations. Could it be that a change of menu is long overdue here?

Perhaps at the next mid-year or end-of-the-year evaluation we could resist discussing either the group's or, for that matter, any individual's failures or successes but concentrate instead on each other's gifts. For example:

On papers prepared for this occasion we write the name of our fellow members in community — a separate sheet for each one.

We spend some time in quiet thanksgiving for each other and in reflecting on the specific gifts each of us has been for the other. We write the most fitting gift of each of our companions on the sheet that bears her or his name. We also spend some time writing down the gift we feel we ourselves bring to community.

After a while, the facilitator or leader of the group tests for *readiness to receive*. As individual members identify themselves we share with them our gratitude for their gifts to us. After our sharing we give them the sheet that bears their name and their gift as a token of our friendship and thankfulness.

Each person whose gifts have been celebrated then shares her or his own insights concerning her or his gifts and reflects with the group how this experience of sharing has been for him or her.

Everyone is celebrated in this manner.

We conclude our sharing with a group prayer of praise or a song and then may wish to share a good meal together or otherwise celebrate further.

Community meetings may benefit also if, in the spirit of holistic values, we precede them with a bit of centering rather than a planned prayer exercise. They will comprise a great deal of speaking as it is. A healthy period of silent focusing on what is going on in each of us would, therefore, be most helpful.[40] If a facilitator or leader were at that time capable of taking us, each in our inner silence, through some of the issues that are uppermost in each of our minds or in our feeling bodies, a great deal of group stress might be averted. It is extremely important that in our meetings we can learn to differentiate our own agenda from the agenda of the group. Focusing can be very helpful here. If the group's trust level is very high a bit of sharing and verbal differentiating of agendas may even be possible, but for most of us silent focusing may be safer at present.

Learning to hold our feelings lovingly, even tenderly and reverently without condemnation, and at the same time being able to differentiate them from the issues under discussion by the group is not an easy task. It is, however, an essential part of healthy group interaction. Jesus was right, after all: Everything revolves around *loving our neighbor as we love ourselves.*

QUESTIONS FOR FOCUS, REFLECTION, AND DISCUSSION

I / Awaiting the Dawn

1. Do you experience religious life today as in crisis? What are the signs of this crisis as you see them?

2. What are the questions emerging for religious life today? Around what issues specifically do they concentrate for you?

3. What is your reaction to the "transformative elements" drawn up in 1989 by the Leadership Conference of Women Religious and the Conference of Major Superiors of Men? Do you think they are realistic? Can you pledge yourself to them? Do you want to do so?

4. Do you see religious life today as prophetic? If so, how so? If not, why not?

5. What has been your experience of living community "participatively, with healthy personal and interpersonal relationships, intentionally, and inclusively"?

95

6. Have you experienced alienation in community? If so, how so?

7. Do you find yourself personally in a growth crisis? If so, how does this crisis manifest itself to you?

8. How do you relate to Bruteau's description of "masculine consciousness"? How prevalent is it in your experience? Where are its advantages for religious life?

9. What has been your experience of group interaction? Has the facilitation been "functional" or "artistic"? Have you felt that your truth was able to appear? Has the facilitator honored the depth agenda of the group?

10. What insight can you draw from the parallel presentations of growth in personal, cultural, and religious consciousness? Where do you see yourself, your congregation? How do you see your own developmental possibilities?

2 / Honoring the Process

1. What efforts is your community (are you) making to give attention, time, and energy to the developmental process in your midst?

2. What factors in your community experience of the past may have fostered regressive behavior in your midst? What do you see as the causes of stress in your life presently, in community life generally?

3. Is independent thinking fostered in your community today?

4. How do you communicate? Do you treasure direct communication? Do you practice it? What do you expect from your leadership in this respect?

5. Can you identify subtle signs of dependency displayed in your local community, in your congregation, by you? Do your congregational gatherings, your community meetings manifest the behavior and language of in-built dependency?

6. "When people have not learned to interrelate with each other, to address personal issues in personal ways and individual issues in private settings, community meetings can become battlegrounds where all possible aggression is dumped either overtly or through passive manipulation." How do you react to this observation? Have you experienced what is described here?

7. "When persons have not learned to acknowledge their inner needs, let alone address them, they unconsciously find someone to blame for their frustration." Does community life suffer from such projections? Is scapegoating a reality in our midst?

8. What is your reaction to the invitation to discover and embrace the shadow material in your life? What hidden positive energy might your shadow have in store for you?

9. "We simply do not all agree about what community is, nor do we all have the same needs in community." What

are your hopes and expectations regarding community life? What needs can you realistically expect to have met in community? How do you react when others' views on this topic or others' needs differ from yours? Can you agree to disagree? Is there such a thing as a right answer here? Do we need to discuss this issue in our local communities?

10. What do you understand by pastoral leadership? What are your expectations from your congregational leadership?

11. What is your reaction to the suggestions concerning direct communication and mediation made to leadership in this chapter? Would this kind of policy further growth among us?

12. Have you experienced the stress of "level skipping" discussed in this chapter? Where do you see level II operative in your life? Has a strong sense of personal identity been fostered among the members of your congregation? How do you understand the dynamic between self assertion and yielding?

13. Have the vocabulary of our communal documents and the concepts of interdependence portrayed there truly penetrated our lives? If so, how? If not, why not?

14. Have "reverse oppression" and a subtle return to tribalism as described in this chapter been operative in your models of decision making? If so, how?

15. Do you sense the need for us to "align who we are with what we say" and to own our brokenness in regard to

the prophetic quality of many of our documents? Do we need time to reflect on the meaning of the values we proclaim in these documents?

16. "Cohesive groups are those that arise around shared understandings, while fragmented groups tend to be those characterized by multiple realities." What does this statement contribute to your understanding of living in community? Is it true that "though we can share our perspectives," we may discover that "we cannot necessarily live together indiscriminately anymore."

17. What would your reaction be to a congregational chapter that would call you to the acknowledgment of your own poverty, recognize the destitution of our times, invite you into questions, and ask you to abide in waiting — in the pain of transformation?

3 / Relational Justice

1. "Personal growth and social concerns are not mutually exclusive. . . . 'Fundamental to social disorder is the disorder within each of us and . . . a re-ordering of society depends upon a re-ordering of individual lives.'" How relevant is this observation to our lives together? Is it true that our very lives *are the mission?*

2. "Relational poverty is currently unidentified, undefined, and unaddressed — much less redeemed. Yet relational poverty and the injustices on which it is built are the sources of unmitigated suffering and chaos."

Is this observation, made by psychiatrist Barbara R. Krasner, true for us? Do we suffer from an inability to reconcile our "impulse toward liberation" with our "impulse toward obligation"?

3. What in your life speaks to the impulse toward obligation? Is there anything in your past that you can identify as particularly conducive to the development of a strong sense of obligation?

4. What in your life speaks to the impulse toward liberation? Do you feel empowered there? Do you feel guilty?

5. What are your regular patterns of relating? Can you honestly say that you love yourself in your differences from others? Do you love others in their differences? Do you love your neighbor as you love yourself? What does that look like for you?

6. How is your childhood upbringing affecting your present relationships, modes of interacting? Do you see any connection there, any need to celebrate or to mourn the past and to set yourself free from its influences?

7. "Identity is achieved at least initially through separation and exclusion rather than through the inclusion that is so often seen as the lifeblood of community." How can the legitimate need for liberation discussed in this chapter prove problematic for community life? What has been your experience here? How does "nihilation" manifest itself in your life, in your community?

8. "Whatever our communal and individual reasons with respect to living arrangements may be, . . . a *conscious*

acceptance of them on our part is most important. If . . . religious life is in transition, then the more aware of it we are, the freer we are in it. Aimless drifting into diverse lifestyles is not responsible adult behavior and speaks of the clan's enslavement to fate." What have you done individually or congregationally to choose your present and your future in this regard?

9. How intensely do you see yourself attached to the "advanced stages of individualization" discussed in this chapter? Does functionality claim you, your congregation, or is it loosening its grip? What signs do you see to support your response?

10. Is the "loss of meaning in religious life" being felt by you as a painful reality or have you adjusted to it and accepted it as normal?

4 / The Love of Christ Impels Us

1. Do you experience yourself, the members of your congregation, as *impelled by the love of Christ?* What does this statement mean to you?

2. A radically new vision is vibrant, alive, and in flux. It often is risky. It flows from experience more often than from speculation. Can we realistically surrender ourselves to such a vision for our future?

3. How can we personalize the Gospel in our lives? How can we regain the passion of our founders? Where have

our congregational or our personal attempts at "re-founding" been true *revolutions?* Where have they been mere *rebellions?*

4. Where in our communal experience have we seen deliberate movement from over-againstness to mutual affirmation, from personal or congregational preservation and enhancement to releasement and an acceptance of mutuality and the intercommunication of "creative love energies"?

5. Have we personally moved beyond "external compassion" to "internal compassion"?

6. Has your understanding of covenant been influenced by reading this chapter's description of participatory consciousness? If so, how so?

7. "We honor diversity even as we uphold community." In the light of the reflection offered in this chapter, what does this mean for us?

8. Our culture's gospel exhorts us to "look out for number one." How prevalent is individualism in our midst? How is it visible even in our collective (institutional) behavior patterns? Could it destroy our founding charism?

Conclusion / Some Thoughts for the Now

Reading the conclusion of this book may open up several avenues for reflection. What are your thoughts on the following excerpts?

a. "It may not be possible for a new group to engage realistically in high-level goal setting at the beginning of the year or whenever they first come together. . . . It may be wise to limit initial meetings of the group to the bare essentials of living space maintenance and leave deeper philosophical commitments for much later."

b. "Often we tend to judge the availability of others by our own and can then easily feel 'neglected' or not cared about when others are not able to be with us during our free time."

c. "Faith sharing requires trust; it requires 'sniffing-out time,' regardless of our congregational at-oneness and 'common' charism."

d. " 'People have no more time to understand anything. . . . Words are the source of misunderstandings. . . . One must observe the proper rites.' "

e. "We are, whether we like it or not, an aging group with the legitimate needs that go with aging. To deny this is simply to be unrealistic and to impose guilt where guilt ought not to be felt."

f. "There is a sensitive balance between being about the *mission beyond one's gates* and being about the *mission within*."

g. " 'Sniffing each other out' . . . requires a great deal of time. It becomes near to impossible when local communities turn into grand central stations. Only time will provide the chance for the shedding of our personas, the lowering of defenses, the nurturing of friendships, and the building of a home."

h. "Religious, too, have space needs ... [and] they are becoming ever more noticeable today.... Adult bodies need adult space, and adult psyches do so as well."

i. " 'That's it, isn't it? It has everything to do with kindness.' "

j. "Perhaps at the next mid-year or end-of-the-year evaluation we could resist discussing either the group's or, for that matter, any individual's failures or successes but concentrate instead on each other's gifts."

NOTES

I / Awaiting the Dawn

1. For an in-depth discussion on the nature of crisis see Fritjof Capra, *The Turning Point* (New York: Simon and Schuster, 1982), chapters 1–4; Barbara Fiand, *Living the Vision* (New York: Crossroad, 1990), chapter 1; for an understanding of crisis in individual development: Bernard J. Boelen, *Personal Maturity* (New York: Seabury, 1978), chapters 4–6.

2. Numerous studies have, in this century, addressed this issue. For greater detail see Richard Schacht, *Alienation*, 1970; many of the works of Erich Fromm, especially *The Sane Society*, 1955; Hannah Arendt, *The Human Condition*, 1958; a book of essays edited by Eric and Mary Josephson and entitled *Man Alone* (New York: Dell, 1971); Rollo May, *Man's Search for Himself*, 1953, *Psychology and the Human Dilemma*, 1967, and many others; most of Victor Frankl's books, especially *The Will to Meaning*, 1969.

3. Material for this analysis was taken largely from Bernard J. Boelen, *Personal Maturity* (New York: Seabury, 1978), a source that has, I believe, become a classic on this subject, and from Beatrice Bruteau, "Neo-Feminism and the Next Revolution of Consciousness," *Anima* 3/2 (Spring 1977). The graphs are personal adaptations of Boelen, *Personal Maturity*, pp. 11, 16, 56–57.

4. Edward C. Whitmont, *The Symbolic Quest* (Princeton, N.J.: Princeton University Press, 1978), p. 221.

5. Genia Pauli Haddon, *Body Metaphors* (New York: Crossroad, 1988), p. 3.

6. Ibid.

7. Bruteau, "Neo-Feminism and the Next Revolution of Consciousness," p. 3.

8. Pauli Haddon, *Body Metaphors*, pp. 3, 4.

2 / Honoring the Process

9. Sandra Schneiders, *New Wineskins* (New York: Paulist, 1986), p. 247. This family model is the one into which we are born, where we are children and depend on our parents to take care of us and make all significant decisions for us.

10. Mary Wolff-Salin, *The Shadow Side of Community and the Growth of the Self* (New York: Crossroad, 1988), p. 25.

11. See Marilyn Wussler, S.S.N.D., M.S., "Don't Is a Four Letter Word," *Human Development* 10/1 (Spring 1989): 19.

12. For an illustration of this I refer the reader to Barbara Fiand, *Releasement* (New York: Crossroad, 1987), pp. 28, 29, where the dream encounter and communion experience with a group of severely deformed women offers not only a good example of the shadow, but also identifies the inner healing possible when this dark companion is accepted and embraced.

13. Here it may be of value to point out that intense admiration of and fascination with another's virtues may also indicate repressed material — this time, a lack of awareness of one's own goodness, which is then projected onto others. A great service would be rendered us if the recipient of our projection could gently hand it back to us, pointing out to us our own goodness.

14. John A. Sanford, *Evil* (New York: Crossroad, 1981), pp. 61, 62. Chapter 5 of this book is an easy reference for information about the shadow and help in detecting it.

15. Ibid., p. 53.

16. Erich Fromm, *The Heart of Man* (New York: Harper Colophon Books, 1968), p. 143.

17. Gareth Morgan points out in his work *Images of Organization*: "Cohesive groups are those that arise around shared understandings, while fragmented groups tend to be those characterized by multiple realities" (p. 133; cited by Mary Jo Leddy, N.D.S., during her address "Leadership for Transformation," given to the Leadership Conference of Women Religious in Spokane, Washington, August 23, 1990, p. 2).

18. Ibid., p. 2.

3 / Relational Justice

19. Barbara Fiand, *Living the Vision* (New York: Crossroad, 1990), p. 62. The quotation cited here comes from Ann Belford Ulanov, *Picturing God* (Cambridge, Mass.: Cowley Publications, 1986), p. 15.

20. Barbara R. Krasner, "(On Relational Justice) Essay I," *Foundations* 20 (October–December 1977): 334.

21. Alice Miller, *Prisoners of Childhood*, trans. Ruth Ward (New York: Basic Books, 1981). Miller's book addresses itself specifically to therapists.

22. Some of the causes for dysfunctional family settings are frequently beyond anybody's control: excessively large and unplanned families, too narrow a time gap between siblings, war, poverty, among others, can all be major factors in childhood deprivation.

23. Courses on human maturation, on the philosophy and spirituality of the person, and on mid-life spirituality deal specifically with issues such as these.

24. Rollo May, *Man's Search for Himself* (New York: Delta, 1953), pp. 125–36.

25. Ibid., p. 127; italics added.

26. That is, playing the child forever, being the care-taker forever, allowing oneself to be the scapegoat in the group, demanding to be provided for, sulking and pouting when one does not get one's way.

27. Life in common does not necessarily equate with life in community. The latter requires the skills for relational living implied by authentic maturity. Today much of what could previously be avoided due to the rule of silence has surfaced and needs to be addressed. This may not be possible for everyone.

28. Leddy, "Leadership for Transformation," p. 12.

4 / The Love of Christ Impels Us

29. Fiand, *Living the Vision*, p. 85 (italics added).

30. To be distinguished from Genia Pauli Haddon's "participational" consciousness of level I, and associated there with the "participation mystique" of the clan. There is in Bruteau's *partici-*

patory consciousness no absorption but a sharing instead, a sharing that recognizes individual uniqueness reaching out and receiving.

31. Discussions on this topic abound. I refer the reader specifically to Elisabeth Schüssler Fiorenza, *In Memory of Her* (New York: Crossroad, 1989) chapters 4 and 5. For specific relevance to religious life today see a comparison between the dualism of early Christianity's Greco-Roman worldview and the mystical tradition of the Jesus movement and beyond provided in chapter 1 of Fiand, *Living the Vision.*

32. Bruteau, "Neo-Feminism and the Next Revolution of Consciousness," p. 1.

33. Fiand, *Releasement,* p. 66.

34. Ibid.

35. Bruteau, "Neo-Feminism and the Next Revolution of Consciousness," pp. 11–12.

36. Ibid.; italics added.

37. Fiand, *Releasement,* p. 66.

Conclusion / Some Thoughts for the Now

38. The word "intentional" as it has been used in this book refers to living communities of choice in whose formation all members deliberately participate. It ought not to be confused with the sociological interpretation given this word by Patricia Wittberg, S.C., in *Creating a Future for Religious Life* (New York: Paulist Press, 1991).

39. Antoine de Saint Exupery, *The Little Prince* (New York: Harcourt, Brace & World, 1971), pp. 83, 84; italics added.

40. I am referring here to Eugene T. Gendlin's technique of focusing that identifies the body as a great source of wisdom and of healing for the entire personality. See Eugene T. Gendlin, Ph.D., *Focusing* (New York: Everest House, 1978). For a more religious interpretation of the same see Ed McMahon and Pete Campbell, *Bio-Spirituality: Focusing as a Way to Grow* (Chicago: Loyola University Press, 1985).